Walking Thru

A Couple's Adventure on the
Pacific Crest Trail

Michael Tyler

ISBN: 978-1-7929-8544-7

Are you interested in hiking the
Pacific Crest Trail? The PCTA is a
great organization with plenty of
information. You can find them at
PCTA.org

dedicated to Margo

Contents

Prologue

In December 2017, a couple of less-than-pleasant things happened, and my reaction to those things led to one of the most satisfying experiences of my life. The first of these events was my 49th birthday. That, taken by itself, isn't much of a milestone. But, turning 49 meant that the following year I would turn 50. I was barreling full speed towards the half-century mark. I had to do something significant to celebrate that milestone.

The second event was a diagnosis of degenerative arthritis in my right knee. I knew my knee hurt before the orthopedist gave me that diagnosis, but I'd always sort of assumed that if I was consistent with yoga, if I strengthened the surrounding muscles, if I babied it, eventually it would improve. But the orthopedist made it clear that my knee was on its last legs, so to speak. To hear him talk, I was at the top of a slow descent into immobility. I took that to mean it was time to check off whatever items I had on my bucket list that required knees.

I've been an outdoorsy person most of my life, and the idea of a long hiking trip has always appealed to me. If my knee was going to leave me incapacitated eventually, it was now or never. I wasn't too interested in the Appalachian Trail; it seemed to have little of what I enjoyed about being outside (sweeping views and solitude), and lots of what I didn't enjoy so much (lots of people and walking through forests). I'd hiked sections of the Pacific Crest Trail in the past, mainly the more popular sections in my home state of California, but stringing the entire trail together into one long journey would be something else entirely.

It turned out that the year I turned 50 was also the 50th anniversary of the official designation of the Pacific Crest Trail (PCT) as a national scenic trail. That designation is admittedly arbitrary. Work began on linking a trail system that would become the PCT in 1932, and the trail was officially completed in 1993. So in reality, the official designation in 1968 doesn't hold a lot of meaning. But, when searching for cosmic signs to justify a passionate pursuit, you take what you can get. The 50th anniversary of the official designation coincided with my 50th birthday, so I didn't have to squint too hard to convince myself that hiking the PCT to celebrate my 50th year was destiny.

But would it be smart to take on such a long journey with knees on the cusp of giving out? What if I started hiking and my arthritic knee shut the whole endeavor down a few days in? A major part of doing a long hike like the PCT is organizing your life in such a way that you can leave it all behind for 5 months. For me, that would mean moving out of the house I was renting with my wife, Margo, putting all of our stuff into storage, and releasing myself from as many commitments as possible for a 6 month stretch. If I put in all of that effort, including giving up a place to live and becoming homeless, only to find that my knee couldn't take the strain a couple of weeks in, I would be devastated, frustrated, and homeless.

I had retired a year earlier, which makes arranging to be away for 5 or 6 months a lot easier. Margo, on the other hand, was still in the midst of her career. Taking time off would be a bigger deal for her. But she's always been adventurous, and she was in a good spot career wise to take a break. So, I thought there was a decent chance I could convince her to join me.

"It's time to make a firm decision," I said to Margo, one evening in early January, as we were cooking dinner together in our home in the San Francisco suburbs. "If we're doing this PCT thing, we need to commit to it and start the preparations in full force."

"I really want to do it," Margo replied, "but I'm concerned. What if we put all our stuff into storage, I quit my job, and your knee gives out two weeks in?"

"That's a huge concern," I replied. "But I'll do everything I can to get it into shape. I'll do training hikes, gym exercises, whatever it takes. I'll even wear that stupid knee brace for the entire hike."

"If you wear a knee brace all the way to Canada,

you're going to have some crazy tan lines," Margo observed.

"Hey, if I have to get crazy tan lines for a once in a lifetime trip, I'll do it," I replied. "That's a small price to pay."

"Do you think I'll have a hard time finding a job when we come back?" she wondered.

"I don't think it would be too hard," I replied. "The economy is booming, and unemployment is at historically low levels. It should be a great time to be looking for a job. Plus, we can go wherever we want. I'm not sure I want to come back to these suburbs after our hike."

"Me neither," Margo replied. "But where would we go?"

"Let's just figure that out later. After all, we'll have all summer to figure out where we want to live while we hike."

We talked it out like that for 30 minutes or so, and suddenly, out of the blue, Margo said, "OK, I'm in. Let's do it."

I don't remember exactly what in the conversation brought her around to such a sudden, firm conclusion, but I didn't question it for a second.

"All right," I said. "It's on."

Over the next several months we did everything we could to prepare. We got together food that we would package up and mail to ourselves as we hiked along the trail, so we wouldn't always have to rely on small town grocery stores for all of our food. We started a regime of training hikes to make sure our legs (and my knees) were up to the challenge. We automated whatever bills it was possible to automate and extracted ourselves from as many of our local obligations as we could manage.

The whole endeavor seemed like an enormous risk. There were the real risks of not being able to finish, of going through all the life restructuring and winding up injured early on. The fear of jumping into something unknown only compounded this. We had no clear sense of what our life on the other side of this trip would look like.

But in exchange for taking that risk, it seemed there was a big potential upside. Everyone has heard that hiking the PCT can be transformational. After spending lots of time outside over the course of my life, I had a good handle on what it felt like to sleep outside and to spend all day hiking with a backpack on my back, so I didn't expect any major transformations. I just wanted my arthritic knee to hold up long enough for me to enjoy the experience. But as it turns out, I underestimated the PCT in almost every way possible. Hiking the PCT was one of the most rewarding and transformational experiences of my life.

Michael Tyler

Part I: The Desert

Chapter 1: It Begins

T he four of us stood in the middle of a flat patch of light brown dirt, compressed to a surface as hard as asphalt by plenty of hikers' feet. Tough, scrubby desert plants punctuated by rocky outcroppings stretched as far as the eye could see in every direction. Bushes with sharp thorns, known as cat's claw, surrounded the open patch of dirt where we stood. In the distance the long, spindly arms of ocotillo cacti poked upwards, along with yucca shoots poking into the sky with their dried flowers on top. The sky was a deep blue, cloudless from horizon to horizon. The temperature was pleasant. We couldn't have asked for a nicer day to start our journey. It was April 7th, 2018.

To the south of us, a rusted, sheet metal wall ran along the Mexican border. In the middle of the dirt patch where we'd parked sat "the monument", a set of pillars that marks the southern end of the PCT. A similar set of pillars sat on the Canadian border, 2,650 miles to the north. That was our ultimate goal, but it was a very,

very long ways off.

My mom and dad had met us in San Diego for two purposes. The first was to see us on our way, and my dad planned to hike the first mile with us to help send us off in style. The second was to take my car, which Margo and I had driven down from San Francisco, and keep an eye on it for the next 5 months.

"This is it," I said, looking around at the dry, foreboding landscape around us. "There's nothing to do from here but walk."

Margo looked around nervously at the desert scrub, and I could see the worry in her eyes. Despite the beautiful weather, I have to admit it wasn't the prettiest piece of wilderness I'd ever seen. In fact, I'd put in the running for the ugliest. But we'd come this far, and there was no turning back. All she said was "All right then, let's hit it."

"Away we go", my dad chimed in. I got the impression he only wanted to get his mile done and then get out of this rather dreary piece of wilderness.

The three of us touched the Mexican border wall, turned north, and took our first steps on the adventure of a lifetime.

That night, Margo and I set up our first camp in a rocky patch of dirt surrounded by cat's claw and low, bushy trees. There was a little stream a hundred yards away, and it was the only water in the first 20 miles of the hike. It was 4 miles from the Mexican border. With over 2,600 miles to hike that summer, we figured we needed to average something like 19 miles each day to make it to Canada. Four miles was a weak start.

Actually, we had decided that our best strategy was to ease into the hike, treating it as the long, drawn out marathon-of-a-hike it was. I worried about my arthritic knee bringing the trip to an early end, and I wanted to give it every chance to strengthen before I pushed it too hard. So, even though we reached our first campsite at 2pm, and we were both eager to get the adventure fully underway, we found the willpower to call it an early day on that first day.

"First day of our hike done," I told Margo. I'd just put up the tent, and she was going through her pack, trying to figure out how best to organize it.

"Yep," she said, "we're on our way. Only two thousand....AAAAAAAAAH!" A scream swallowed the end of Margo's sentence.

"What?" I said, spinning to face her, searching for what had startled her.

"That," she said, pointing over towards the edge of our campsite, where a 4 foot snake was slithering through the dirt up against a rock. It didn't have a rattle on the end of its tail, which in the southern California desert means it's not poisonous.

"Our first snake," I replied. I picked up a rock and threw it in the snake's direction. I missed by a foot, but it was enough to cause the snake to slither off into the scrubby brush. "I bet it won't be our last."

After dinner, we sat outside our tent watching the shadows grow long as dusk settled in. The air was still warm, but the beginnings of a chill were settling over the desert. The mountains on the horizon reflected the orange of the sunset.

"I can't believe we're actually doing this," I said. "This is going to be our life for the next 5 months."

"I can't believe it either," Margo replied. "I wonder what the next 5 months will be like."

"I'm not sure," I replied. After a minute of silence, I added, "I'll bet it will be a relaxing, fun adventure. It might even change the way we look at the rest of our lives after we're done."

"Maybe," Margo said. "We'll find out."

We had no idea what we were in for. We'd read books and blogs by others who had hiked the trail as part of our planning and preparation. We'd joined Facebook groups where others who were hiking the trail this year connect, and get advice from people who have hiked it in the past. But even with all that, I couldn't imagine what it would be like to live outside for 5 months, to spend time living in some of the nation's most beautiful wildernesses. At that point, in that conversation, we vastly underestimated the impact the trail would have on us both.

"I'm getting chilly," Margo said. The temperature was dropping quickly as darkness set in. "It's only 8:30, but I think I'm going to get in my sleeping bag."

"I'm right behind you," I said.

We both slept a deep, relaxing sleep under a clear, starry sky. The temperature dropped overnight, as it often does in the desert, but our sleeping bags were more than capable of handling the mild temperatures. After months of planning, it was happening. Our PCT hike was finally, officially under way.

The next morning, we woke up with the sun. The air had cooled down overnight, and it was tough to pull myself out of the warm, downy comfort of my sleeping bag. After a leisurely breakfast, we packed up our stuff and got ready to start our first full day of hiking on the PCT. Our four mile day yesterday had been easy and fun, but four miles a day would not get us to Canada before the snow flies in late September or October. If we were going to make it, we needed to pick up the pace. So today our goal was to get to Lake Morena, the next water source. It was about 15 miles away — still not quite the 19 miles we'd need to average, but it seemed like a good goal for day two.

The scenery got better as we hiked through that first full day, which made us both feel better about the whole endeavor. The scrub brush that had been ubiquitous for the first few miles from the border gave way to more interesting and varied plants. We saw more cactus, sometimes in crazy shapes, sometimes with bright flowers nestled in among the sharp spines. The long, spiky arms of ocotillo cactus reached up into the air, with their red blooms giving a splash of color to the desert earth tones. We rolled along, up to the tops of ridges and down into the valleys in between. As we walked up onto a rise early that morning, the views opened up. We could see for miles in every direction. Brown, barren looking peaks lined the horizon and ridgelines out to the east. Yucca stalks shot up out of the brush, stretching towards the cloudless blue sky. Looking ahead, we could see the brown, dusty stripe that was the trail cutting through the landscape, undulating over the rolling topography. There was no sign of civilization anywhere out here.

"Well, that's not quite what I expected from the desert," Margo said as I caught up to her on top of a rise. As I looked ahead, I could see the trail drop down into a gorge and come back up steeply on the other side. "I thought 'desert' meant flat and sandy. You know, like the pictures you see of the Sahara. That's some serious up and down."

"No kidding", I replied, still out of breath from the climb up to the ridgeline. The endless ups and downs in front of us looked intimidating, especially with the heavy packs we had on our backs. "But check out that view. No sign of civilization as far as the eye can see. This is our home for the next 5 months." It was an exciting realization that gave me butterflies.

"I guess it's time to get used to it," Margo replied.

We continued on for another hour or so until we came on a couple standing in the middle of the trail. The guy was in his late twenties, with bright red, unkempt hair and a thick, unruly red beard to match. He wore purple shorts and a lime green shirt. He was the exact opposite of the muted earth tones that surrounded him.

"How's it going?" I asked as I came up behind them.

"I just saw my first rattlesnake!" the brightly colored guy exclaimed.

"Your first on the trail?" I asked, "Or your first ever?"

"My first ever!" he said, still very excited. "I came around the corner and almost stepped on it, before it slithered away. There it is, right there." He pointed to the ground right next to the trail. There it was, just watching us lazily in the sun. The most disconcerting part was how relaxed the rattlesnake seemed about us. He wasn't coiled up to strike, wasn't rattling, and clearly wasn't scared of us. This was an animal that knew its place on the food chain, and that place was at the top.

"Whoa," I said. "That's a beast. That's the first rattlesnake we've seen on the trail. By the way, my name's Mike, and this is Margo."

"Nick," the guy said. Indicating the woman with him he continued "and this is my wife, Jam."

"It's a pleasure to meet you guys," I say. "Are you guys heading to Lake Morena today?"

"Yep, that's our plan," Nick replied. "What about you guys?"

"Same plan. I guess we'll see you there."

"Yep, we'll see you," Nick said, and with that he and Jam headed off down the trail. Margo and I hung around for a few more minutes watching the rattlesnake watching us, then we headed off on our way.

Late that afternoon, as we hiked along a rocky ridge, we spotted a large grassy campground ahead on the desert floor, next to a large, shallow lake. It was Lake Morena, our destination for the day. After a long day of hiking through dust and dryness, we were thrilled to see an actual lake. We'd walked fifteen miles through the desert that day, down into deep washes and up onto high ridgelines. Our packs felt heavy on our backs. In fact, they felt heavier and heavier and heavier as it got later and later in the day. Eventually we would get so used to carrying these packs that we would forget they were on, but we weren't there yet. We were tired, and ready to put down our loads.

We walked through the large campground, following signs directing us to a designated PCT campsite, set back away from the car camping spots. When we arrived, there were about 15 people there already. Some were working on setting up their camps, and others were milling about, chatting with each other. The sun was still high in the sky, and the air was warm and comfortable.

"Hi", I said to a guy in his mid-50s sitting at the picnic table, messing with a water filter. "How does this work? Can we camp anywhere?"

"Sure, anywhere over there on the grass," he replied, with a slight European accent.   "That green tent over there is mine. My name is Tommy, by the way." He stuck out his fist for a fist bump.

Personal hygiene habits vary among people hiking the PCT. Some people are fastidious, but no matter how hard you try you can only stay so clean when you live in the dirt with limited access to water. As a result, most people hiking the PCT lie somewhere on the hygiene spectrum between questionable and downright disgusting. One way that hikers deal with this potential risk is to never shake hands with anyone, but to fist bump instead. I guess the theory is that fewer germs live on your knuckles than in your palm. In any case, fist bumping is the norm on the PCT, and we embraced it. We wouldn't shake anyone's hand for the next 5 months.

I returned Tommy's fist bump. "I'm Mike, and that's my wife Margo, looking for a campsite over there". I pointed towards Margo, scouting out the grassy field for a flat spot.

"Pleasure to meet you," Tommy replied. "I'm sure I'll see you around."

Maybe he would, and maybe he wouldn't. I had heard the Pacific Crest Trail Association (PCTA) issued something like 4,000 permits that year to people hiking long distances on the PCT. They spread those permits out over a couple month period, so there's no way we would meet everyone hiking that year. But we would run into many of those people during our hike. Some of those people we met we'd see them regularly for the next 5 or 6 months. But, if a person is moving at a slightly different pace than we were, we might meet them and never see them again. Or perhaps we'd meet them once and not see them again for 3 months, 1,500 miles down the line. We'd be meeting a lot of new people. It would be a lot to keep straight.

In the meantime, Margo had scoped out a spot on the grass next to Nick and Jam. I walked over and started setting up our tent. Nick and Jam didn't have a tent set up, but instead had a large tarp spread out on the grass, with their sleeping bags set on top of it.

"No tent for you guys?" I asked Nick. He was still wearing his same obscenely colorful outfit from earlier in the day. Actually he, like the rest of us, would wear the same outfit every day for the next several months.

"Not tonight," he said. "We're cowboy camping." Cowboy camping is thru hiker lingo for sleeping without a tent. It's a popular way to sleep, especially when there are no bugs around and no chance of rain, as was the case tonight.

"That sounds like fun," I said, although I was imagining rattlesnakes and scorpions slithering into a warm sleeping bag on a cold night. "Are you carrying a tent at all?"

"Yeah, we've got one," Nick replied. "But I came out here to be outside. In fact, I've got a goal of cowboy camping every single night through the desert." His wife, Jam, rolled her eyes at this.

"That's a noble goal," I replied, not sure of what else to say. "You too, Jam?"

"No," she said. "I don't mind cowboy camping tonight, but I plan on sleeping in the tent plenty going through the desert. Nick's got his own agenda."

I'd later find out that Nick had a couple of other goals he was working towards as well. He was trying to make it through the desert (700 miles, 5 or 6 weeks) without pooping outside. He would try to make it to a real toilet, or at least an outhouse, whenever nature called. This sounded particularly challenging since there would be stretches several days in length where we wouldn't see anything like an outhouse or toilet. He also went through one stretch with the goal of doing a "candy resupply", meaning when he resupplied in town, he only bought candy, and that was all he would eat for the next 4 or 5 days. It was almost like hiking 2,650 miles in a summer wasn't enough of a challenge; Nick had to add in some additional rules to keep it interesting. I was getting the strong impression that he marched to his own beat, and I liked him immediately.

"Are you guys using any apps on the trail so far?"

Nick asked.

As more and more people have hiked the PCT in recent years, and as smart phones have become ubiquitous, a couple of smartphone apps have been developed that help out with the hike. These apps let you know if you're on the trail at any given moment, which is really nice to have. But even more importantly, they have things like water sources and campsites marked on them, and you can easily see distances to those places. I don't think I met a single person hiking the PCT who didn't use at least one of those apps, and most people used two.

"I've been using Halfmile and Guthooks," I responded, "but it seems like Guthooks is a lot better. What about you?"

"Same," he said. "I didn't realize how important those apps were going to be, but I'm using them like constantly. Knowing where water is, especially here in the desert, is going to be crucial."

"Yeah," I agreed. "And knowing where the good campsites are is useful too. Imagine if your phone dies, you wouldn't be able to see any of that."

"No doubt," Nick agreed. "I need to get some sort of battery so I have some backup."

"Yeah, me too. It's going to be important to keep our phones charged on this hike, it seems like."

Throughout the evening, we met everyone camped at the lake, and chatted at least briefly with each of them. We remembered as many names as we could, since we never knew who we would see down the trail. But out of the 15 or so other people we shared our campsite with that night, we'd only ever see 3 again. Such is the nature of a long hike.

The first few days of our hike were through the lower elevations of the southern California desert. It's a beautiful stretch, going up and down over rolling hills. Brown mountains covered with rocky outcroppings loomed on the horizon in all directions. The browns and dark greens of the desert were occasionally punctuated by wildflowers, sometimes displaying themselves in wide yellow or red swaths that covered entire hillsides. It was very pretty. We heard many other hikers talking about being surprised at the richness and beauty of the desert.

Even in those early days, we got into a rhythm. Margo and I split up the chores involved in setting up and taking down our camp each day. When we got to camp, I'd set up the tent, and Margo would track down some water and make dinner. We quickly got efficient at our routine, and it took on a strange domestic quality that I hadn't anticipated.

On the fourth day, we began our first significant climb up to higher elevations. Until that point we'd been going up and down constantly, as my legs would attest. But so far, the rolling hills never led to any significant altitude gain before the trail turned back downward. Now we were heading consistently upwards towards Mt Laguna.

Mt Laguna sits on a small ridgeline that separates San Diego and its eastern suburbs from the dry, unpopulated, starkly beautiful Anza Borrego desert to the east. The ridgeline is only about 5,000 feet above sea level, far from the highest elevations we'd see on the trail, but it's high enough that it's a stiff climb up out of the desert. We powered through switchback after switchback, gaining elevation and watching the plant life change from desert scrub to something that was more alpine, with plenty of pine trees and oaks.

As we approached a switchback, we saw a guy leaning on his poles, catching his breath. "Tommy", Margo said as she recognized who he was, "How are you doing?"

"Great," said Tommy, breaking into a huge grin. "It's so nice to get up into the mountains a little, to see some trees around."

"Yeah, no kidding," I agreed. "I like the desert, but the cool air and the forest is a nice break. It smells so fresh up here." The pine scent was intense after days of hiking through cactus and cat's claw.

"I'm just happy to be up away from the rattlesnakes for a while," Margo added. We hadn't run into another rattlesnake since the second day, but we'd heard plenty of other people tell stories of being surprised by them.

"What's your plan for today?" I asked Tommy. "How far are you going?"

"Well I've got to pick up a resupply box at the Post Office, and then hopefully I can get a few miles past that," Tommy responded.

"Same," I said. "We'll see you up at the Post Office."

I had started working on the resupply boxes right

after we'd made the final decision to start hiking. There are two ways most people handle getting food, or resupplying, on the PCT. One approach is to plan everything ahead of time and mail food to strategic spots along the trail. This is obviously some work. In fact, it turned out to be a lot more work than I was expecting. You've got to decide where to send food, and how much to send to each spot. You've got to buy all that food in advance. Since most post offices won't hold a package indefinitely, it's helpful to have someone to mail your boxes a couple weeks before you expect to pick them up. It's what you could call the hard approach.

The much easier approach is to just buy food in towns along the way. There's really no planning required before you start the hike. You just show up at the Mexican border and start walking north, buying food as you go. If you get sick of something, you just don't buy it anymore. You don't have to pay for shipping on all those boxes full of food you'd be mailing to yourself using the hard method, which adds up to a surprisingly substantial amount. The disadvantage to this much easier approach is that some of the trail towns we'd pass through had tiny grocery stores, sometimes even less stocked than a typical 7-11. In those cases, we'd lose a lot of flexibility in our meals. I'm not talking about the kind of flexibility where you substitute bacon for pancetta, or having to go with rice instead of quinoa in your stir-fry. Hardly. By lack of flexibility I mean we would have to go days at a stretch eating nothing but ramen noodles, dehydrated potatoes, and Fritos.

I'd started experimenting with dehydrating my own food for backpacking trips a few years earlier, and I generally liked the results. I liked to make dinners loaded with dehydrated vegetables. I figured we'd be missing fresh fruit and veggies a lot while we were out hiking, and I thought making dinners that were loaded with vegetables would help to satisfy that craving. I also wasn't sure I wanted to explore the long term health impacts of a Frito-based diet. I was, after all, turning 50. Fritos for dinner is a young man's game.

In the end we decided to go with a hybrid approach to resupplying. We prepared boxes full of dehydrated food and trail snacks for about half of our planned resupplies, about 15 boxes total. For our other resupply stops, in larger towns with better grocery stores, we'd rely on those grocery stores. Hopefully the grocery stores would be big enough that we could avoid having too many ramen noodle and beef stick dinners. We thought this approach would give us enough variety that we wouldn't get sick of the food we mailed to ourselves, because half the time we could buy stuff that was completely different. It turned out to be a bad compromise, one of many lessons we learned on the trail.

At the post office in Mt Laguna we were picking up the first of our resupply boxes. We were only 4 days into our hike, and really still figuring out the way everything was going to work for the rest of the summer. But we knew we were excited about getting a resupply box. Even though I'd just finished packing our boxes a week and a half earlier, I had already kind of forgotten what wound up in each box. All I knew for sure is that it would be food, mostly high calorie food, and with our hunger kicking in, that was enough.

We got to the Mt Laguna post office right around lunchtime. There's a general store – something like a 7-11, but with less variety and more fishing gear – that shares a porch with the post office, so it was a popular hangout for PCT hikers. People and packs were lined up along the porch. Small piles of astoundingly stinky socks were scattered about next to people poking at blisters small and large on their feet. People were opening the boxes they'd just picked up, reorganizing their packs, chatting with other hikers, and generally enjoying themselves. The sun glowed in the clear blue sky, warming the pine scented air. Everyone was smiling.

"I'll go grab our box from the post office, you scope out a place to sit and go through it", I suggested to Margo. When I came out with our box, I saw Margo in the shade of a tree at the edge of the parking lot. I headed over.

"We got it," I said. "Box number 1, picked up without a hitch."

"It feels like Christmas! Let's see what's in it". Margo looked at the package with anticipation.

"OK", I said, as I ripped the tape off the box. "Let's see… dehydrated beans, spaghetti… oh, look, a bag of sesame sticks!" Sesame sticks were our favorite trail snack, at first.

"Oh, and Goji bars!" Margo spotted her favorite

brand of energy bar.

We divided everything up, each of us excited about the great food that we had and the delicious meals to come.

"Hey guys," Tommy walked up, carrying the box he'd just picked up from the post office. "Mind if I join you?"

"Have a seat," I said, and Tommy plopped down in the dirt and went through his box as well.

We ate a lunch we'd gotten out of our box, and slowly other hikers came over and joined our little circle in the shade of the tree. Nick and his wife, Jam, who we'd met at our first rattlesnake sighting on day two, joined us. A few other people who had just picked up resupply packages also came over and went through their booty.

"Hey, does anyone want some Clif bars?" a guy sitting next to me asked.

"Yeah, I'll take some Clif bars," someone else responded. "Anyone want oatmeal packets?"

After a few moments of silence, the guy next to me said "Throw them in the hiker box."

Hiker boxes are a wonderful concept. In places where hikers tend to congregate, such as outside this post office in Mt Laguna, someone places a cardboard box. Anyone who has something they no longer want to carry, but which someone else might want, will put that thing in the box. It could be food, or a piece of gear, toilet paper, socks...almost anything. Everyone then knows that whatever is in the box is free for the taking. There are hiker boxes at virtually every stop along the trail. Some hiker boxes are better than others, and one of the things hikers will discuss with great passion and interest is where the good hiker boxes are located. But whether a box is good or bad, one thing you can always find in a hiker box is oatmeal. Always. Just about everyone who hikes the PCT gets sick of oatmeal sooner or later.

We would take advantage of hiker boxes throughout the spring and summer, getting a little extra food when we needed it, leaving some behind when we felt over loaded. For the most part, they were a huge help in our hike. There was one unusual occasion when the hiker box actually complicated our hike, but that was still a ways down the trail.

We spent about 2 hours that afternoon sitting under that tree, in a shaded patch of dirt, talking with fellow hikers. Time didn't seem important. We had nowhere to go that day other than to our next camp, which, let's face it, was wherever we wanted it to be. We had nowhere particular to be the next day either, or the next, or the next. The spring and summer stretched out before us, seemingly to infinity. There was nothing to do but this - enjoying time with our newfound friends on this trail that was our new home. It was the most unhurried, relaxing, pleasant two hours I can remember spending in a long time. It would be a feeling I would get used to over the summer.

"What a sweet spot!" I said as we walked down to the beach. A couple we had met the day before, Jake and April, had set their tent up on a wide, sandy beach that bordered a shallow stream that meandered by. Leafy green trees lined the stream and surrounded the beach, creating a nice oasis from the desert we'd been walking through all week. It was getting close to the end of the day, and we were looking for a campsite. "That sand looks really comfortable. Mind if we join you?"

"Of course, make yourself at home," Jake replied. "I think it's only about a mile from here to Warner Springs, so we'll have an easy day tomorrow get to town."

"That sounds great," Margo replied. Warner Springs would be our first stop in a genuine town on the trail, just over a week into our hike. "We haven't had a shower since we started, so we're due. And we haven't resupplied since Mt Laguna, so we're almost out of food. A shower and a huge meal... "I can't wait."

I headed off to look for a spot to pitch the tent, and Margo chatted a little more with Jake and April.

As I was putting up the tent, I noticed Margo staring intently at the bushes about 30 feet away. April noticed it too.

"Awww, look at the cute bunnies," April said, following Margo's gaze towards the bushes. On a second glance, I saw a little group of rabbits nibbling on grass at the edge of the beach. They were adorable.

"They'd look a lot better in my tummy," Margo said, still staring intently at the cute rabbits. I didn't see that coming, and the look in her eyes made it clear she wasn't joking around. She wanted to eat a bunny.

Stunned, we all turned to stare at Margo. You have to understand, Margo is a very sweet, kind person. Everyone she meets likes immediately, and she never consciously hurts others. No one expected her to be talking about eating bunnies. That was way out of character.

"What did you say?" I asked.

"I said those rabbits look delicious," she replied. There wasn't a hint of irony on her face, no indication that she was joking around. Just an intense, hungry look.

April laughed, then Jake and I joined in too. "I never would've expected that from you, Margo, April sputtered between laughs. "You're normally so sweet."

"Yeah, well, I'm hungry," Margo said matter-of-factly.

That night, we gathered for dinner on the soft sand between our two tents. The conversation followed what we were learning was a typical thru hiker conversational path; lots of talk about what we were going to eat in Warner Springs, some in depth discussions of upcoming showers and laundry, and other things that we normally take for granted, but already somehow feel like decadent luxuries. Eventually the conversation turned to trail names. None of us had a trail name yet, but many of our friends were starting to get them.

There are a couple of general rules of etiquette about trail names in the hiker community. It's widely understood that someone else has to give you your name, and it should be based on something unusual or unique about you. Appearance, behavior, an article of clothing; anything is fair game.

"You know," April said, "I have a trail name for Margo."

"What is it?" Margo asked.

34

"Well, remember how she was hunting those innocent little bunnies earlier? She turns from a sweetheart into a predator in a flash. I think we should call her werewolf."

"I love it!" I say as I laugh loudly.

"That's perfect!" says Jake.

"What do you think, Margo?" April asked. "Are you good with werewolf?"

"I love it," Werewolf replied.

"Look, they have a pack scale," Margo said. We'd just arrived at the Warner Springs community center, where they really roll out the red carpet for PCT hikers. The center is open to hikers all day, with places to charge electronics, hot and cold drinks, and snacks that kind locals bring in. About thirty tents crowded the large yard next to the community center. And there was a backpack scale hanging from a tree in the yard. "I really want to know what my pack weighs."

"Me too," I said. We hadn't picked up our resupply in town yet, so our packs were at their lightest, devoid of food and water. It was a perfect time to weigh them. It would tell us our base weight, or the weight of our packs without all the consumable stuff that varies from day to day. Along with food, base weight is one of the main conversational topics among PCT hikers.

Margo hoisted hers onto the scale. "Sixteen pounds," she said. "Wow, it feels like a lot more."

I slipped the hook through my pack strap and checked the dial. "Same here," I said. "Sixteen pounds."

Ten years ago, sixteen pounds would have been a great base weight. But, as equipment manufacturers make gear lighter and lighter, the average pack weight falls. Sixteen pounds is probably about average for PCT hikers in 2018, but there were people at the scale who had base weights below ten pounds, and some as low as seven pounds. That's right — a tent, sleeping bag, clothes, whatever you need to cook meals — all of that clocking in at under ten pounds. It's really amazing how little stuff you need to get by in the wilderness.

"I need to make mine lighter," Margo said. "By the end of the day it always feels so heavy."

"Well, when we get to our room tonight," I said. "you can just lay everything out on the bed and figure out what you can do without." We'd booked a hotel room for the night. Margo and I had made an agreement before the hike that we'd try to sleep in a hotel room once a week so we had a chance to get clean and feel a little more normal at least occasionally. We were 9 days into our trip, so we were overdue for our first hotel stay.

"A room," Margo replied, a broad grin creeping across her face. "What are we doing hanging out at the community center? Let's go take a shower."

The amount you appreciate a shower is proportional to the time since you had your last shower. It had been 9 days since our last shower, so this one felt phenomenal. Warm steam filled the bathroom. The desert grit turned the water a dark brownish-red as it swirled down the drain. The scent of the soap was strong, almost overwhelming. It was the first artificially scented thing I'd smelled in days.

When I came out of the shower, Margo had the contents of her pack spread across the bed. There was a small pile of stuff off to one side. "That's not coming with me," she said, indicating the pile.

"What are you giving up?" I asked.

"Mostly extras of stuff. An extra pair of underwear, two extra shirts that I don't need. And this shampoo, it's just too heavy."

"Wow," I said. "I'm surprised, I have to say." We were only 100 miles in, and Margo was ready to go ahead in full PCT minimalist fashion. After she jettisoned the pile, the only clothes she'd have would be one shirt, one pair of shorts, and a hiking dress for town stops.

"The weight is killing me," she said. "I feel every extra ounce on the trail."

"I know," I replied. "Especially at the end of a long day."

"Well, hopefully this will better. Now I'm going to enjoy that shower."

"You're going to love it," I replied.

Lying down on the hotel bed that night, with its clean sheets and its soft mattress, felt wonderful. The clean sheets smelled of laundry soap, and the soft mattress yielded in a way that felt so much better than sleeping on the ground. And yet, I had trouble falling asleep. I missed the starry sky, the clean air, the sound of the birds and crickets. I missed being outside. I didn't know it at the time, but that longing would only grow as we made our way north.

Chapter 2: Southern California Mountains

We were nearly two weeks into our hike. Over those two weeks, we'd camped in a different spot every night, always with other PCT hikers. It seemed that we were in synch with a group who was keeping the same pace we were, so we kept seeing the same people again and again. Every night there was a slightly different configuration of people at our campsite, most of whom we'd met before, but some of whom were brand new. The previous night, we'd camped up on a ridge in the San Jacinto mountain range, less than a days hike outside of the town of Idyllwild. We shared our camp with a guy in his 50s we'd met a few days earlier who went by AWOL, a pair of women in their early 20s from Orange County, and a couple of young, ambitious mountaineering types from Switzerland. The last forecast we'd seen had predicted a storm was moving in overnight, and the wind that had picked up outside our tent overnight confirmed it.

"Are you ready to get up, Margo?" We were still laying in our warm sleeping bags, listening to the wind ravage the tent. Even from within our sleeping bags we could tell it was cold in the tent, which meant it was going to be *really* cold out there in the wind.

"No," Margo replied. She'd never been a fan of the cold, or of mornings for that matter. I couldn't blame her. I wasn't exactly fired up about going outside into that wind either.

"Me neither, but we should get down off this ridge before this storm gets even worse. I'll go make some coffee. That'll warm us up and get us moving."

"OK." I could tell she wasn't completely on board. But we couldn't just hang out in the tent all day. I put on my clothes as quickly as I could and got out of the tent.

It looked like all of our camp mates were still in their tents, probably waiting for the brutal wind to die down before getting up and braving the cold. One of the Swiss guys, who went by the name of Ranch, was in a tent that was completely collapsed on the ground around him. He was still inside, but the tent was just lying on top of him like a tarp, with no support from poles or anything else. The outline of his body looked like a shrink-wrapped toy, still in its package. It wasn't the way tents were supposed to work.

"Hey Ranch, are you OK?" I quietly asked as I walked over to the puddle of nylon.

"I'm OK," came back a deep, heavily accented voice from under the tent.

"What happened to your tent?" I asked. It looked

like it had blown over during the night.

"The god damn tent was rattling like crazy in the wind," Ranch replied, somehow sounding both sleepy and agitated. "It wouldn't shut up. I couldn't sleep, so I took the poles out. It's quieter this way."

Makes sense, I guess. I left Ranch to his nylon cocoon and went about making coffee.

As soon as the coffee water had started to boil, Margo was up and out of the tent. It was cold up on that ridge. The wind howled up above the trees, and even in the relative shelter of our little campsite there was a stiff breeze. Gazing upward at the dark clouds moving in, it looked like the worst might still be to come.

"Looks pretty gray," Margo said, looking up at the sky. "Something serious is coming our way."

"Yeah. Let's get packed up and get down out of here."

We alternated between drinking coffee, eating breakfast, and getting all of our gear packed up and ready to go. Over the last two weeks, we'd gotten efficient at packing up our gear. We had a system, we each had our roles, and in no time we were ready to go. We left camp silently before anyone else was up out of their sleeping bags.

As we headed along the trail, the wind proved to be blowing even worse than we anticipated. The little grove of trees where we had camped had provided quite a bit of shelter. When we left the sheltered campsite and got out onto the exposed ridgeline, the icy wind whipped fiercely past us, occasionally threatening to blow us off our feet. We also got a broader view of the sky, and it did nothing to reassure us. Black clouds swirled to the west, looking ominous.

"Let's get down off this mountain as soon as we can," Margo suggested.

I looked at Guthooks, the PCT mapping app we'd been using, and said "It looks like we can cut down off the ridge to the road in about in a mile. From there, we can hitch into Idyllwild."

"Perfect, let's do it."

Just as we got to the junction where we were planning to head to the road, the snow started to fall. There were just a few flakes blowing in the wind at first, but gradually more and more snow swirled around us. Eventually it was a full on blizzard, and we could only see 20 yards in front of us through the swirling snow. This was late April in southern California. It's not an area or time of year that you normally associate with snow. We had just the right clothes for hiking through a warm desert, but we were unprepared for a blizzard. We put on all of our clothes and headed down the mountain, hoping for shelter from the wind as we got down below the ridgeline.

As we descended, the storm continued to pick up steam. Everything was covered in rime ice, giving everything a white, wintery pallor. The ground was turning white as the snow accumulated. The sky was a dark gray as the wind churned a solid layer of clouds above us.

It was amazing that just yesterday, the sky had been blue and clear, and everything around us had been brown and green, earth tones as far as the eye could see. Now it was all transformed to a world completely cloaked in white. It was actually really pretty, but we weren't hanging around to enjoy the view. It was cold and wet, and it was only getting colder and wetter. There are times for pondering the majesty of nature, and times for getting the hell out of it. This was the latter.

We spent the next hour walking down towards the highway. As we got lower, the snow continued to pick up momentum. Finally, just as my hands were beginning to go numb in the cold, we reached the highway. We were about 10 miles out of Idyllwild, and our plan was to hitch hike into town from here. It took about 2 minutes before a nice lady from Idyllwild stopped and picked us up.

"Are you guys hiking the PCT?" she asked as we threw our backpacks into the back of her SUV.

"Yep, we are," I replied. "We started out on April 7th, so we're about 2 weeks into the trip now."

"Wow, good for you guys. This weather is unusual. You were smart to come down off the mountain."

"It was pretty crazy up on top there," I said. "The wind was out of control." We were sailing down the highway, happy to be out of the weather for the moment.

"Like I said, this is an unusually late storm for us," our kind driver replied. "Normally it's nice this time of year. This is hiker season in Idyllwild. We love to see you guys pass through, and I like to do whatever I can to help out."

As if to prove her point, she hit the brakes at the sight of a couple other people up ahead on the side of the road. "Do you mind if we stop and pick up some others?"

"Of course not," Margo replied. "The more the

merrier."

By the time we got into town, every seat in the SUV was taken, with a couple of people riding on others' laps. It turned out lots of people were coming down off the ridge to get out of the storm, and they were all looking for rides into town. This kind woman crammed as many PCT hikers as she possible could into her car, doing all she could to help us out.

"Let me show you around town," our driver announced as we pulled into the little village of Idyllwild. "Here's the campground where a lot of hikers stay, and over there is a pretty decent pizza place. Around the corner here is a fabulous brewpub, and I think they'll give you your first beer free if you're hiking. Oh, by the way, it's taco Tuesday at the Mexican place down the road. Best $1 tacos you've ever had." She continued to drive around the center of town, kindly pointing out everything the town had to offer, then dropped us off where every hiker coming into town wants to go first – the post office.

Everyone thanked her effusively as we got out of the car and headed into the post office pick up our resupply box.

One thing that would amaze me throughout our PCT hike was the unbelievable kindness of the people we would meet along the way. This ride from a kind woman on a stormy day would be the first of many examples of that. She didn't have to pick us up, she didn't have to cram her car full of people who hadn't showered in several days, and she certainly didn't have to give us a tour of her lovely town. But she did all of those things, and she did them with no expectation of anything in return. It was an unconditionally generous act.

We would learn over the course of the summer that the PCT isn't really something you can do alone. You have to rely on help from others, and most of those others are strangers. Trail angels, who provide help and support to PCT hikers, provide a lot of that support. Sometimes they'll hand out food at remote locations, sometimes they'll give people rides into town, and some will even let people stay at their house. People who live in towns near the PCT are used to seeing hikers trying to hitch hike into town from the trail and are very generous about offering rides.

I have had a strong independent streak my whole life. I've always tried to make sure I could take care of myself, that my reliance on others was minimal. But on a hike like this, you wind up relying on the kindness of strangers often. You really have no choice in the matter. What surprised me about this hike, perhaps more than any other aspect, is how generous people could be, how unselfish and giving. In the spring of 2018, our society felt especially fragmented, deeply divided on even the most basic of questions, with a general sense of malice pervading seemingly everything. And yet, here we were, receiving help from strangers, with absolutely no ulterior motive or incentive outside of a desire to help. It was unexpected and wonderful. It reminded us that people are good, and we would be reminded that again and again as we hiked north.

"Over here," Giancarlo called to us from down the street.

"Is this the spot?" I asked as we walked in his direction.

"Yep, dollar tacos." Giancarlo and Tommy were just outside the front door of a Mexican restaurant in downtown Idyllwild. This was the place with the dollar taco deal that the woman who drove us into town had told us about. We were starving, and loading up on cheap tacos with some newfound friends sounded like a great way to spend the evening.

We had met Giancarlo a week ago in what was easily our most unpleasant camp site so far on the trip. That night we slept underneath a highway overpass in the Anza Borrego desert, trying to use the base of the overpass as a break from the biting wind that blasted particles of sand at any exposed skin. "My name is already on the list for a table."

We spent a few minutes catching up with Giancarlo and Tommy, all of us describing that morning's storm, and how we had got down off the mountain and into town that afternoon. It was still pretty chilly out, especially as the sun was setting, but at least the snow had stopped. We were planning on spending the night in a campground in town and heading out early tomorrow morning to get back on the trail.

As we settled into our table and scanned the taco menu, I asked "Are you guys going to the top of San Jacinto tomorrow?" San Jacinto is a peak that sits about 4,000 feet above Idyllwild. Its summit is over 10,000 feet, making it among the highest peaks in southern California. The summit itself isn't on the PCT, but there's an alternate route that goes over the summit. It adds several miles to the hike, so some people skip it.

"Not me," replied Giancarlo. "I'm going to keep moving ahead."

"I'm thinking about it," Tommy said. "You guys?"

"We're taking the detour," I said. "I've been up there, and it's totally worth it. You should join us."

"Sounds good. Count me in." Tommy was always interested in side trips and extra adventures. He was in great shape even before the hike had started, so the physical effort wasn't too much for him. Since he had come all the way from Denmark, I got the impression that he wanted to see as much as he could on this thru hike.

"All right, we'll meet you at the shuttle stop at 8am," I replied. "What kind of tacos are you guys ordering?"

The tacos were wonderful, and they were a steal at a dollar each. Our hiker hunger was kicking in. We demolished more than our share of large, tasty tacos, and chased it down with Mexican beer. As we finished our dinners, the talk turned to the mechanics of the trail. Miles per day, rest days, resupply strategies, and finally, annoyances on the trail.

"Have you guys seen any poison oak or poodle dog bush yet?" Giancarlo asked.

"We haven't seen either one yet," I replied, "but I know I'm super-sensitive to poison oak. I've had these systemic reactions. Sometimes I'll get a little on my hand or something, and a few days later it will have spread to my whole body, including places that I know were never exposed. It's so itchy, and I get these big, weepy blisters. I hate that stuff. I avoid it like the plague."

"It's nasty," Giancarlo agreed. "I haven't seen any poison oak yet, but I saw some poodle dog bush back in the lower desert." Poodle dog bush is a flowering plant that only exists in California and Baja, generally at moderate elevations in the mountains. It's got a toxin that causes a reaction similar to poison oak. It's a different toxin from the one poison oak produces, but the rash is just as persistent and unpleasant.

"Yikes," I said. "I haven't noticed any yet, but I'll keep my eyes open. I've never had poodle dog bush rashes before, but I don't want to find out how strongly I react to them." Later on, I would get all too familiar with my reaction to poodle dog bush.

We talked a while longer about people we'd met on the trail, and the logistics of the next section. It was getting dark outside, and we were all adjusted to the typical hiker schedule that had us in bed by 9pm, and often earlier. So Margo and I bid the others farewell and headed out to our campsite in the park to shiver away the rest of the evening.

The summit of San Jacinto was just as glorious as I'd remembered. The views were absolutely stunning. The peak rises up from the desert above Palm Springs, looming 10,000 feet over the city below. Looking to the east the desert towns surrounding Palm Springs were visible far below us. To the north, the San Gorgonio mountain range dominated the horizon, with the snow-covered peak of San Gorgonio capping it off. To the northeast is the lower desert range that separates the high desert of Joshua Tree National Park from the lower deserts. To the south and west, lower scrub-covered mountains stretch as far the eye can see. The sky was clear and blue, and there wasn't a cloud in sight. Even at almost 11,000 feet, the temperature was warm and pleasant at mid-day. It was a gorgeous day, and we had a stunning view. We found a nice spot to sit on the summit, took off our shoes, and broke out our lunch.

"What do you think of this?" I asked Tommy between bites of peanut butter smeared tortilla.

"Unbelievable," was Tommy's reply. "You know, before this hike I had never hiked a day in my life. The only time I slept in a tent was in my backyard, just before coming over to start this trip. I have to say, this is amazing."

"Wait, you came here from Denmark, planning on living outside all summer, and you'd never been camping before?" I was pretty stunned.

"I saw a German documentary about the PCT, and I decided I wanted to do it," Tommy replied. "I guess I thought I'd just kind of figure it out as I went."

"Wow, that's incredible!" I was amazed. I'd spent lots of time backpacking over the past couple of decades, so I had a feel for what I was signing up for. Tommy had come in blind.

"How do you like it so far?" Margo asked.

"I love it," Tommy replied. "I'm seeing such beautiful views every day, and I really enjoy the physical aspect of it too. It's everything I thought it would be."

"Do you think you'll keep doing this kind of thing

after you're back home in Europe?" Margo asked.

"Oh, no way," Tommy replied. "Not a chance. Once this is done, I'll never sleep outside again."

I searched Tommy's face for a hint of irony, a signal that he was joking. But he was completely serious. Tommy seemed to be looking for something specific from the PCT this summer, and if he found it on the PCT, there would be no reason to sleep on the ground another night.

We chatted on the peak for a couple of hours, soaking in the warm sun and the endless views, and just enjoying ourselves. As the sun moved lower in the sky, it became clear to us all that we had to leave this little oasis.

"It's getting late," I offered. "Let's go down until we get to some water and set up camp for the night. Tomorrow we'll have to do the big descent, so we should rest up."

From here, the trail would drop down all the way to the desert floor, 10,000 feet below us, in about 25 miles. That was the big descent. It was the part of the hike that I was most concerned about, given my bad knee. Descents are the hardest on bad knees, and a 10,000 foot descent is just about as brutal as it gets. I was nervous.

The next morning, we woke to clear skies and great views out across the desert. We were camped at the top of the ridgeline that would take us down the mountain to the desert far below. We could look all the way down to the desert floor from our campsite, and it was a long way down. It looked intimidating.

"This is it," I said to Margo. "If my knee can make it down this hill, I'll feel a lot better about our chances of making it Canada."

"You'll be fine," she said as she scooped up a spoonful of oatmeal and guided it to her mouth. "I have complete confidence. That knee brace seems to help out a lot." Her smile was reassuring, but I wasn't so sure. I had been wearing the knee brace every single day so far, and it really seemed to be doing its job. It seemed like my knee was feeling better the further we walked. But I didn't have to tell Margo what would happen if my knee gave out. We had quit our jobs and put all of our stuff into storage. We were just over two weeks into the hike. If we had to quit hiking, we'd be left with nowhere to go and nothing to do for the rest of the summer.

"Good morning," Tommy said cheerily as he walked towards our camp, his pack all packed up and on his back. "Did you guys hear about the bees?"

"Bees?" Margo said. "What bees?"

"I just heard there's a hive of bees about halfway down the mountain on this ridge. There's no way around them, and apparently they're aggressive. They've stung a few people."

"Great." I'd been worried about a knee injury, and now I had to worry about a swarm of killer bees on top of that. "Every day is an adventure on the PCT, I suppose." Margo and I finished loading the rest of our gear into our packs, and the three of us headed out.

The descent towards the desert floor started out beautifully. Being on such a sharp ridge with dramatic drops on both sides, we had spectacular views down to the desert for the entire walk. Every time we went around a corner, the views would change, each as spectacular as the last. Finally, we arrived at the place rumored to have the bees.

"This is it," said Tommy, stopping in the middle of the trail. The three of us had stuck together that day, the better to navigate the potential challenges. Here the trail was built along the side of a rocky cliff. There was a 30 foot wall to our left, and a 50 foot sheer drop off to our right. There was no way of passing through here except on the trail. Somewhere just ahead in that cliff, a swarm of mean bees had taken up residence.

"What's our strategy?" I asked.

"I say we all stick together and just go through as fast as we can," Margo suggested. "That seems like the best bet to me."

"I agree," said Tommy.

"OK, Me too," I added. It seemed like as good a plan as any.

We started walking along the trail, staying within arms reach of each other, and everything seemed fine. Then I heard a buzz. Then another. Within seconds, a persistent buzzing surrounded my head. Bees were swarming. They were flying into my ears. They were getting stuck in my hair and under my hat. They were everywhere. I walked faster. The buzzing grew more intense. I could sense more bees joining the swarm around my head. I started to panic. I swatted at the air with my arm, then swung my arm and hand wildly around my head.

I felt a sharp sting in my neck.

Then, as quickly as it started, the buzzing ended. The

surrounding air was silent once again. I guess I had gotten far enough past their hive, and they'd decided to leave me alone. I touched my neck where the bee stung me and felt a welt already rising up there.

"How is everyone?" I asked, turning to look at Tommy and Margo behind me. They were both still close by, safe from the buzzing swarm.

"I'm fine, no stings," said Margo.

"Same here," said Tommy.

"They got me," I said. "Right on the neck."

"Let me see," Margo said, drawing her head close to my neck. "Oh, yeah, I see where it got you. It's swelling already."

Tommy pulled a small pill out of his pack. "Take this. It's an antihistamine. It should help with the swelling, and maybe with the stinging too."

Meanwhile, Margo had pulled a pair of tweezers out of her pack. "Hold still," she said as she gingerly raised the tweezers to my neck.

"Ouch!" The growing welt on my neck was pretty sensitive.

"Got it!" Margo exclaimed. There it was, a tiny stinger pinched between the end of the tweezers. It's amazing that something that small can hurt so bad.

After recapping our rush through the bees and having a little snack, we continued on down towards the desert floor. As I walked, I thought about my encounter with the bee. I had only suffered a minor little sting, nothing to get worked up about, but to deal with that the people I was hiking with had immediately come to my aid. Tommy had pulled the antihistamine out his first aid kit immediately, and Margo had set straight to work on removing the stinger. I'm sure they would have done more if I had needed anything else. It was really a minor thing, but still it warmed my heart. Just like trail angels, other hikers on the trail are generous, kind and helpful. It's just the way people treat each other out here. During that descent, I thought about how lucky I was to be surrounded by that kind of energy. We all were.

Eventually we made it down that long descent. My knee held up fine. In fact, it felt downright strong. The more I walked on it, the stronger it was getting. At this rate, I'd be 100% healed by the time we got to Canada.

That night we camped with Tommy at the bottom of the descent, down on the desert floor. It was the first night in a week or so that we'd been down out of the mountains at such a low elevation, and the temperature that evening was downright balmy compared to what we were used to.

After setting up our tents, we all gathered in a patch of dirt between the rocks and cacti to cook up our dinners. "It's so nice to not be freezing at night for a change," I said as I waited for a pot of water to come to a boil. "It's great to just be able to relax in shorts and a T-shirt."

"I love it," Margo replied. She's not a fan of cold weather, and she'd been suffering a bit through the last week at higher elevations.

"Enjoy it while it lasts," Tommy threw in. "Soon we'll be heading up into those mountains over there." He pointed across the valley floor to the San Gorgonio range, which formed a foreboding wall several miles away, on the other side of the freeway.

"The scenery was wonderful going over San Jacinto," Margo said. "I hope there's lots more like that ahead."

"It was nice," I agreed, "but there were a few too many trees for me. I'm not a fan of hiking through forests like that."

"I don't know," Tommy looked puzzled. "Those trees up there on the mountain were pretty, and unique too. They don't grow like that down lower. They're interesting, even if they do get in the way of the views."

"And being in the trees is soothing," Margo continued. "It just makes you feel at ease."

"I guess," I replied. I wasn't totally sold. "Trees are nice, but epic views are, well, epic."

That night, as the sun set on the warm desert evening, Margo and I climbed into our tent without the rain fly. We would pay the price for such a pleasant evening later. But for now, lying in our sleeping bags, we watched the peaks ringing the valley turn from granite gray to alpenglow orange as the sun fell further below the horizon, then to black as the sky darkened and night set in. The clear sky was studded with an amazing number of stars, brought out by the dark night and the clear desert air. As I lay in my sleeping bag looking up at them, I was completely, deeply relaxed. The PCT was just starting to work its magic on me.

"I can't believe how hot it is out here today," I said as we plowed through the deep sand. We were crossing the flat desert between the two large southern California mountain ranges, San Jacinto (the one we had just climbed) and San Gorgonio (the one we were heading towards). On top of those peaks it was no doubt cool and pleasant today, but down here on the desert floor between them it was a scorcher.

"I hope I have enough water," Margo said. "I'm going through it pretty fast this morning."

"I'm kind of low too," I said. "There's supposed to be a stream in six miles or so, we just have to make it that..." I was cut off mid-sentence by a loud rattle just in front of me. I froze, paralyzed by some deep-seated evolutionary reaction to the buzz of a rattlesnake. The snake slithered across the trail about ten feet in front of me, eyeing me aggressively while it shook its rattle, clearly very agitated.

"That scared the crap out of me," I said, as the snake, still rattling, slithered under a nearby cat's claw bush. My heart was racing, adrenaline was pumping through my veins.

"Yeah, me too," Margo replied. "My God, that's a scary sound."

We continued down the trail. It's nice of the rattlesnakes to give a warning when you're near them; it's certainly preferable to them just attacking your calf in silence. But those warnings are terrifying. Now, as I walked, I feared every rock on the side of the trail, every bush that we walked past, harbored another potential viper. For the next hour, I was convinced that another snake would jump out at any moment. Finally, after a couple of miles I was able to relax. And then...

"Holy crap, another one?!?" I declared as another snake rattled at me. Just like the last one, he slithered across the trail in front of me, rattling and eyeing me the whole way.

Meanwhile, in the growing midday heat, both Margo and my water bottles were nearly empty. It was noon, getting hotter by the minute, and we still had another three miles to water.

"We just need to keep moving," Margo said. "If we can get to that stream soon, we can get water, and take a break and wait out the heat a little. You go first," she added. I was rattlesnake bait.

We continued down the trail, hopeful that the next three miles would go by quickly. We would have cool water, hopefully a shady spot for a nice relaxing lunch. Those miles were flying by, until....

You would think that by the time the third rattlesnake did its thing we would have been used to it. Nope. There's something about that buzzing rattle that sends signals straight into your amygdala, and from there your fight of flight system is launched into the stratosphere. No matter how many times you've heard that buzzing, it still lights up every warning system. So after the third rattle, we found a spot to sit down, rest, and try to get our heart rates down.

"How much water do you have left?" I asked, as Margo pulled her water bottle out of her pack.

"Just this," she said, holding up her nearly empty water bottle. "And I'm going to drink it right now."

"I'm out now too," I said, after I swallowed the last of my water. It was close to 100 degrees out here now, the mid-day sun high above us. The landscape looked harsh and threatening. Sand and rocks surrounded us. Scrubby, thorny desert brush was spread here and there between rocks, but there was no water in sight. No doubt there were countless rattlesnakes snuggled up among those foreboding rocks. "I guess we'd better keep moving."

By the time we reached the stream, my throat was as dry as the desert landscape around us. My lips, thoroughly chapped, burned in the desert sun. We found a spot in the shade of a rock outcropping at the stream's edge and drank a liter of water each.

"Wow, what a morning," I said, as we got our lunch out of our packs. "We got rattled at by three rattlesnakes, we ran out of water, and it was by far our hottest day on the trail so far."

"Definitely not the best day," Margo agreed. "I really hate those stupid snakes. I think this has been our hardest day on the PCT so far."

"I agree," I replied. "It's been a tough one. But at least we've got water now. Let's just sit here until it cools off, then get in five or six more miles before we camp."

Our nerves were frazzled. We took a long, much needed siesta as the desert baked in the mid-day heat. By the time we left our little spot by the river in the late afternoon, the air was cooler and the snakes had apparently found something to do besides rattling at us. We had a pleasant walk to our campsite, along the banks of another little stream five miles ahead.

"Do you want some olive oil?" I asked. We were sitting in the small patch of shade thrown by the narrow canyon wall, in a vain attempt to get out of the midafternoon heat. It was almost the end of April now, and the weather was getting noticeably warmer, especially in the middle of the day. We'd fallen into a pattern of taking longer breaks around lunch, trying to be in as much shade as possible during the hot parts of the day.

The narrow canyon was bone dry, but smooth rock formations in the channel indicated where water sometimes flowed during the rainy season. The narrow, rocky canyon walls were lined with various types of angry plants. Cactus, agave and cat's claw were interspersed with sharp, intimidating rocks, giving the whole area a generally foreboding feeling.

"Sure, that sounds great," Margo replied. We had started carrying olive oil on the theory that it was the lightest food that we could get our hands on, in terms of the number of calories per ounce we had to carry. We put it in our dinners, both to boost the calories and to give them a nice richness that always seemed to be missing in dehydrated food. Now Margo was adding it to a tortilla that she had already smeared with peanut butter, making for a real calorie bomb. Have I mentioned how great it was to never have to worry about over eating? Calories were our friends, and we got on friendly terms with as many of them as we could.

We enjoyed a quiet lunch in the shade and rested for a couple of hours. I pulled my Kindle out (a luxury on a hike like this, but one that I wasn't willing to give up), and relaxed as the sun crossed its apex. After our quiet siesta, we packed up and struck out into the afternoon heat.

"Are you ready for a break?" I asked. It was about 5 in the afternoon, and we'd put in several miles after our leisurely lunch. Sunset was late this time of the year, and with our long lunch breaks, we still planned on getting in a couple more hours of hiking before setting up our camp.

"Sure, there's a good spot," Margo said, indicating a rocky overhang that created a patch of shade. Out here, where the tallest vegetation was shoulder high bushes, finding shade was never easy.

We sat down in the dappled shade and each pulled snacks out of our packs.

"Oh shit," I said. "Oh no. This is a disaster!" I was horrified. The bottle of olive oil had come open in my pack. About half the bottle had leaked out into my pack. It seemed that everything I was carrying was slick with oil — tent, sleeping bag, clothes, everything.

"Oh my god," Margo exclaimed, looking at me with horror in her eyes.

"I can't believe this," I said. "This is going to ruin our gear."

The stuff in our packs was everything to us. It was our food, our shelter, our way of getting water, our way of staying warm. It was literally all we had. Without that stuff, we'd be in quite a bit of trouble. To make matters worse, we were in the middle of the desert. There was no water anywhere in sight. Even if cleaning off the oil was as easy as just rinsing it off in a stream, it wouldn't have mattered. We couldn't even do that. Fixing this would not be easy.

"We just need to find some water," Margo suggested. "I have some dish soap. Maybe we can get stuff clean."

I was so angry with myself I could barely speak. I pulled out my phone and checked Guthooks for the next water source. It wasn't easy, because olive oil covered my hands by then, and I had no way to clean them. Eventually I figured out the closest water was at a lake six miles away. We'd have to go there tonight. There really was no choice.

I furiously got my pack together as best I could under the circumstances and wordlessly started walking. Six miles to the next water. Six miles of carrying around a pack full of olive oil. Six miles of the oil slick inside my pack spreading throughout our gear with every step. I walked as fast as I could, just wanting to get my gear clean. Even though it may have been among the fastest six miles we walked on the PCT, it felt like the longest.

We finally hit the shore of Silverwood Lake around 6:30 that evening. Silverwood Lake is a huge reservoir. We'd hit the eastern shore of the lake, but it looked like the lake extended at least a mile to the west. Tomorrow we would hike around the lake, past the big car camping campground on the other side where the road meets the shore, and then onwards toward Canada. But for now, all I could think about was getting the oil out of my pack and cleaning my gear.

I dropped my pack on the sandy beach at the lakeshore and immediately pulled everything out. I laid out the groundsheet we used under the tent every night to keep the sand from sticking to my oily gear, and then threw all the other gear in my pack onto the groundsheet. I assessed the damage.

The tent was pretty bad. I took it out of the bag, stood in knee deep water in the lake, and rinsed it out as best I could.

"Here, take this soap," Margo offered. She'd just

arrived at the beach a few minutes behind me. In my furious walk to this lake, I'd just plowed forward without worrying about where she was.

"Thanks," I said. The soap helped. I repeated the process with my sleeping pad, my clothes, everything that had olive oil on it. The excess oil was easy to rinse away, but everything still had plenty of big oily splotches.

Finally done, I surveyed the gear laid out on the groundsheet on the beach. Everything was wet, and the sun was dipping down towards the horizon. The air was cooling. There's no way stuff would dry before dark.

With everything relatively clean, and my stress and frustration levels declining, I surveyed the beach we were on for the first time. The beach itself was down in a little cove, surrounded on 3 sides by a cliff and one side by the lake. The cliff was covered with graffiti. There was a fair amount of trash on the beach. It wasn't looking like a nice place to spend the night. It was actually pretty nasty.

Margo was noticing our surroundings as well. "I'm not so sure about this beach. Somehow it...oh my god! Look at this!." Margo gestured towards a dead rattlesnake on the beach.

"That's it," Margo said, clearly agitated. "I don't want to sleep here." Rattlesnakes were Margo's biggest nemesis on the PCT. Even dead ones were too much.

"I agree," I said. The dead snake was bad enough, but even beyond that there was something about this beach that left me feeling uneasy. "But what can we do? It's going to be dark soon, and my stuff is all wet."

"What about that campground on the other side of the lake?" Margo offered. "If we can get there, it should be at least a little nicer."

"That's three miles away," I said, "the sun is already starting to set. Do you really think it's worth it? If we do one more mile, it will be our longest day yet on the PCT."

"I don't feel great about this beach."

"Me neither," I replied. "OK, let's pack our stuff up and go."

We both packed up our stuff and got ready for the three mile walk to the campground. Packing up all my wet gear soured my mood even further. This had not been a good day so far, and now we were going to be walking in the dark to our camp, where we'd again have to deal with our wet gear as we got set up.

We left the beach and started hiking around the lake just as the sun dipped below the horizon.

"We've only got three miles to go," Margo said. "We can do that in an hour. If we push it, we should get to our camp just as the last light fades."

"All right, then let's push it," I grumbled. I wasn't at all happy about the way this day was going.

The trail wound along the top of a series of cliffs that ringed the lake, 50 or 100 feet above the shore. Scrubby Manzanita surrounded us on both sides, but it was low enough that we could see in all directions. As dusk settled in, the sky lit up with oranges and reds that were reflected in the lake. The heat of the day was past, and the air felt cool and crisp. It was a great time of day to be hiking, and an absolutely gorgeous mile. Few things can brighten your mood like an unexpectedly gorgeous sunset on a serene lake. I felt more peaceful and relaxed with each step.

We arrived at the campsite just as complete darkness was setting in. We surveyed the large grass yard looking for a good spot to pitch our wet tent.

"Hey guys!" someone was yelling at us from under a pavilion on the other side of the grass.

"Bandit!" Margo cried. "And Mantis! Great to see you guys!"

"Great to see you guys too," Bandit replied. "Want some pizza?"

Hang on. That can't be right.

"You guys have pizza?" I asked, bewildered.

"Yeah," Bandit replied. "And beer. There's a place in town that delivers to this campground. They stop delivering at 8, but we've got leftovers. Have a beer." He held a full bottle of Stone IPA towards me. There was no way I was going to pass that up.

"I can't believe this," I said. "You have no idea how much we need this. Thanks!" I popped the top on the beer and took a swallow. Well, it was meant to be a swallow. That beer lit up the pleasure circuits in my amygdala like a Christmas tree. I felt every swallow radiate through my cells, hydrating them, infusing them with calories. I wanted to savor it, but I just couldn't stop myself. I drank half the beer in one pull. I don't think it's hyperbole to say that was the best beer I'd ever had.

As we finished off the leftover pizza, I told the story of our afternoon. "So now we're going to have to find a spot to pitch our wet tent. In the dark."

"Why don't you guys just sleep under this pavilion

with us?" Bandit offered. It was a huge pavilion, with plenty of space for all of us. It would surely be more comfortable than the tent.

"All right," I replied. "We'll take you up on that."

"The Trail Provides." That's a common saying on the trail, but one that always struck me as a little cheesy. It is meant to invoke the sense of community on the trail, the willingness of people, other hikers and trail angels alike, to help out when help is needed. It's also meant to invoke the idea that an adventure like this is best left at least partially up to chance, that detailed plans are often thwarted. Tonight, that saying didn't seem cheesy at all. Tonight, the trail had provided just exactly what I'd needed. It wouldn't be the last time.

"Thanks for the ride. Can we give you a few bucks for gas?" I asked as we grabbed our backpacks out of the back of the pickup.

"No, no, I'm happy to help out. Just pay it forward one day," the kind gentlemen who had picked us up replied. "Good luck on the rest of your hike."

"Thanks!" Over and over we'd hear responses like these, from generous people who just want to put some good out into the world. Over and over we'd hear of other hikers who had similar experiences, often accompanied by the same comment: "It really restores my faith in humanity". We felt the same.

We had just hitchhiked into Wrightwood, a small town in the San Gorgonio Mountains. A cold fog enveloped the village, a steady drizzle slicked the streets. The town was compact, with a handful of coffee shops, restaurants and bars concentrated in a couple of blocks, and several more blocks of quaint houses surrounding them.

We had decided that we would take our first full rest day in Wrightwood. In thru hiker parlance, a rest day is a "zero day", because you hike zero miles on that day. We had hiked over 300 miles so far, and gone over 3 weeks without a single rest day. We were due, and we were looking forward to it. Really, really looking forward to it. The cold drizzle only made sleeping inside more attractive.

"I think this is it." I gestured towards the apartment above the garage.

"Looks great," Margo replied. "This is going to be so nice."

We walked into the studio apartment we'd booked on AirBnB. Surveying the room, we saw a TV, a comfortable couch, a bed in the corner, and a fully stocked kitchen. Living a nomadic life outside has many upsides, but we definitely missed having a home. It looked like this place had everything we needed to give us the sensation of having a home, if only for a couple of nights.

"I'm not leaving this place until Tuesday," Margo said, as she threw herself on the bed. It was Sunday afternoon.

"All right," I said. "I like that plan. I'll run to the grocery store and get what we need for the next two days."

An hour later, I was back in our little studio apartment with a whole roasted chicken, veggies for a salad, strawberries, a huge watermelon, a bag of apples, and a bunch of grapes. We missed fruit.

"That was just what I needed," Margo said, picking the last pieces of meat off the chicken. "I'm going to cut up that watermelon for dessert."

"It's so nice to have a kitchen," she continued, slicing the watermelon into giant wedges. "A fridge, fresh fruit and veggies... not having that stuff is one of the hardest things about hiking the trail."

I miss cooking too," I said. "When we finish this, we need to get a place with a big kitchen."

"Where do you think that should be?" Margo asked.

"I don't know," I replied. "I don't think I want to go back to the crowdedness and expensiveness of the Bay Area. Maybe somewhere in the desert, like Arizona? I've been enjoying hiking through the desert."

"Maybe," Margo replied, looking hesitant. "I've really liked the desert too, more than I expected. As long as I can find a decent job there, that sounds great. But let's not think too hard about it yet. We've got a long time to sort that out."

"Yeah, we'll have plenty of time to worry about that later," I replied. "For now, let's just enjoy our watermelon."

It was a fabulous watermelon, and a wonderful rest day in Wrightwood. We watched movies, took an unreasonable number of showers, and ate pounds and pounds of fresh produce. All of that probably doesn't sound so luxurious to you, but for us at that point in our hike, it was all that we wanted, everything we could have wished for.

Michael Tyler

Chapter 3. Doctors and Sunburns

We were back to hiking. Coming down out of the mountains surrounding Wrightwood had been glorious. The trail followed a ridge for the most of the first day, giving us seemingly endless views of mountains off in the distance in all directions. The wildflowers were continuing to pop up more and more every day. We would spend hours hiking through a rocky landscape with nothing but browns and greens, and then suddenly come to a hillside completely covered with bright purple and little yellow flowers. We were thoroughly enjoying ourselves.

Our goal on this day was the Acton KOA. Acton itself is a tiny town with little to offer. Its main attraction is running water. There's no water for many miles on either side of the town, so almost everyone hiking the PCT stops at the KOA to rehydrate. The fact that they have a small store (with ice cream) and a swimming pool is enough to convince most people to spend a night there, despite the $20 charge per tent. If there's one thing PCT hikers hate, it's paying for campsites.

We could see the KOA down below, right next to the highway that snaked along the valley floor. It looked miniscule from high up on this ridge. We could see tiny RVs lined up in neat rows, and tents scattered about the expansive yard. But our eyes were pulled towards the gleaming blue swimming pool and the smaller hot tub next to it. It stood in stark contrast to the barren hills surrounding us. We'd managed to dip our feet into some of the larger streams we'd crossed, but this would be the first swim in an actual pool since we started the PCT.

We started walking, our pace a little quicker than normal. I was almost out of water and looking around it was pretty clear there would be none to be found until we got down to the KOA. As always, we were both hungry too, and as always, we were ready to put our packs down for the day and have a relaxing afternoon.

Finally, the trail dipped down off the ridge we'd been following and headed toward the valley floor. We walked into the KOA office at about 3pm tired and thirsty. Our clothes were covered with desert dust and lined with salt stains from days of drying sweat.

In the store, while I arranged our campsite with the clean, perfumed lady working behind the counter, Margo took a quick look around the little store. The selection left a lot to be desired. But there was ice cream and Gatorade, which were both going to really hit the spot after hiking through a hot desert all afternoon. For some reason Margo decided a jar of pickles would be the right thing to round out our lunch and bought that as well. We paid for our campsite, gathered up our eclectic groceries, and went out to find a place to set up our tent.

While I was setting up the tent, Margo set out our groceries along with the lunch we'd been carrying on a picnic table. I sat down, still exhausted and filthy, ready to eat. The pickles Margo had grabbed in the store were especially tasty. In the hot desert, the cool crunch mixed with the vinegary tang of the pickles was incredibly satisfying.

Finally, there was a single pickle floating in the jar of pickle juice. They'd been so good, we'd demolished the entire jar. It was just sitting there in between us, a lonely pickle floating in half a quart of brine. And I thought, "I wonder how that juice tastes..."

I figured I'd give it a sip. After all, if the pickles were so delicious, the juice couldn't be half bad, right? So I picked it up for a sip, just a taste, and....

GULP....

Wow, that was bigger than a sip...

GULP....

Holy crap, this stuff is amazing...

GULP....

Wait a minute, am I drinking pickle juice?

GULP....

71

I placed the empty jar on the table between us. Margo stared at me, mouth agape.

"Did you just drink a jar of pickle juice?" she asked me. She looked more than a little worried.

"Half a jar", I reply, as stunned as she was. I hadn't been intending to down the whole thing, but it was just so delicious. "It was only half full after we ate the pickles," I stammered, as if that somehow made drinking pickle juice reasonable.

I sat there for a minute, waiting for the imminent wave of nausea to overwhelm me. Surely it was coming. I was about to see that pickle juice a second time as it came up the same way it went down.

But I felt great. I'd been thirsty, I'd been sweating out salt all day, and I guess pickle juice was just what I'd needed. I ate my ice cream bar and headed to the shower, feeling energized and happy.

We enjoyed the rest of the afternoon. We spent an hour or so in the pool, alternating between soaking in the hot tub and jumping in the cool swimming pool. There was a group of about 10 PCT hikers enjoying the soak along with us, mostly in the hot tub. Looking around, it was impossible not to notice other hikers' feet. There were lots of blisters, some of them pretty nasty looking. One girl named Milkshake had four giant flaps of dead skin hanging off her mangled feet. It looked like a collection of zombie feet soaking in that hot tub. I guess that's what hiking hundreds of miles through the rough desert terrain will do to feet. I counted myself lucky that my feet, and the rest of my body for that matter, were holding up so well.

It was only after I was clean, dried off, and lying in bed to sleep that night, that I questioned the cleanliness of the hot tub. But they put chlorine in those things, right? How bad could it be?

"I can definitely feel it," I complained. We were up on a high ridge, munching on sesame sticks and almonds as we took one last break of the afternoon. We could see the trail arcing along the ridge the way we'd just came, through the low brush and grasses that covered the hills here. The sun was lowering towards the horizon, and the afternoon was taking on that cool, muted quality that meant the end of the day was getting near. "I think it's swelling a little more."

"Let me see," Margo said, tugging at the back of my shirt.

I turned my back towards her and lifted my shirt up to my shoulder blades. I couldn't see what was there, but I could tell by Margo's long pause that it wasn't pretty.

"It doesn't look too bad," Margo offered after a full 5 seconds of silence. "It's swollen and red, but it doesn't seem to be spreading. Do you want to see it? I can take a picture."

The cyst on my back had gotten infected. This had happened to me once before, years earlier, with a cyst on my shoulder. I'd had that one removed before the hike, thinking that I didn't want a repeat of the problem right where my backpack strap hit my shoulder. Unfortunately, it seemed like I was getting a repeat

73

anyway, just in a different spot.

"No, I don't want to see it. Ignorance is bliss." Deep down, I was terrified of what the thing would look like. I could tell by Margo's reaction that it wasn't pretty.

"What do you want to do?" Margo asked.

"Well, we're still 3 days away from Tehachapi. Going back to Green Valley would take a couple of days, and we'd still have to hitchhike to a doctor. And besides, tomorrow is Friday, so by the time we get anywhere we'll have to wait until Monday to see a doctor anyway. So I guess we just keep going towards Tehachapi, and I'll see a doctor there."

"OK, that sounds good to me," Margo replied. "Does it hurt when you carry your pack?"

"Yeah, but it's bearable," I said. It was bearable, but barely. If it got any worse (which seemed to be pretty likely) it might cross the threshold to intolerable.

Margo happened to have cell service up on this ridge, so I borrowed her phone to make an appointment at a doctor's office in Tehachapi on Monday morning.

The swelling of the cyst got worse over the weekend as we made our way towards Tehachapi. I could tell it was getting worse by the way it felt against my pack when I hiked. With every step, as my pack jostled, the friction on the swollen cyst would give me a little jolt. All those little jolts, step after step after step, were adding up to a fair amount of pain. Margo kept an eye on the infection, checking it a couple of times a day to make sure nothing crazy was happening with it. I could tell by her voice and demeanor after looking at it each time that it wasn't getting better. Again and again, she asked if I wanted to see a picture of the thing. Again and again, I declined.

We got into Tehachapi as planned on Sunday evening, and after a loud night camped in a grassy spot at the airport, we headed to the doctor's office on Monday morning. I was lead back to the examination room, and Margo came along for moral support. A few minutes later, the doctor came in.

"What's the trouble?" she asked as she settled into her chair. A nurse sat at a computer typing in notes into her computer.

"Well, I've got this sebaceous cyst on my back that's gotten infected," I explained. "We're hiking the PCT, and it took us a few days to get to town, so I'm afraid I might have let it go a little longer than I should have."

"OK. Let's get your blood pressure and weight, and then we can take a look," she replied.

I stepped onto the scale in the corner of the doctor's office. "195 pounds," the doctor said. "That's a good weight for your height." I'm 6'4".

"195!?!" I said, shocked. "That means I've lost 30 pounds since we started this hike."

"Thirty pounds is a lot to lose," the doctor replied. "When did you start hiking?"

"April 7th," I replied. "Just over a month ago. That seems like an awful lot of weight to lose in a month."

"It sure does," the doctor replied. "Maybe you should eat more."

In the moment, I couldn't think of a nice way to say "No shit, doc," so I just sat there silently contemplating my dramatic weight loss.

"Let's take a look at that cyst," the doctor suggested, as I sat back down on the examination table.

I turned my back to her and took off my shirt. There was silence in the room. There was not a sound from the doctor, the nurse or Margo for at least 10 seconds. That seemed to be the consistent reaction to seeing this thing on my back, and it left me more than a little concerned.

"You're going to have to go to Bakersfield," the doctor finally said after what seemed an eternity. "You need to have surgery. We can't take care of that here."

"But we don't have any way to get to Bakersfield," I told her. I explained how we were hiking from Mexico to Canada, how we'd walked into town with no car.

"That's just more than we can handle here in the office," she said. "You'll have to figure something out."

My mind was reeling, running through possible ways to get down to Bakersfield. It was 50 miles away, which is a pretty big deal without a car. Maybe we could find a trail angel to take us? Hitchhiking didn't seem like the best plan — hadn't I heard something about Bakersfield being the meth capital of California? I couldn't remember for sure, but I really didn't want to take the chance.

"Hang on a minute." The doctor excused herself from the room, and the nurse followed her out.

"What are we going to do?" Margo asked when we were alone in the room.

"I don't know," I replied. "We have to get this taken care of somehow. I'd rather not have to hitch. Maybe we can get a trail angel to give us a ride down to Bakersfield." I was concerned. I figured once I made it to the doctor's office they wouldn't let me leave until this massive mess on my back was cleaned up. But suddenly it seemed that we had another journey to make before I could get it fixed.

The doctor and the nurse came back into the exam room, trailed by another guy who looked to be in his mid-50's. "This is Dr. Frank," the original doctor said, indicating the new guy in the room. "He thinks he can help."

"Great!" I said. Things were looking up. Maybe we wouldn't have to head down to Bakersfield after all.

"I'll just lance it and drain it," Dr. Frank said. "We'll have you on your way in 5 minutes."

This was great news. When I'd had the infected cyst on my shoulder this is exactly what they'd done, and it's not a big deal. It doesn't get rid of the thing permanently, but it gives it a chance to beat the infection, which meant we'd be able to continue our hike.

"All right," I said. "Let's do it."

"OK," Dr. Frank replied. "I'll be right back." The two doctors and the nurse left the room. About 30 seconds later, the nurse came back and opened the door 3 or 4 inches.

"What is that about?" Margo asked. "Do they think we stink?"

"That must be it," I say.

The doctor came back in, along with the nurse. They left the door wide open. So we stink. Whatever.

Dr. Frank gave me a shot of anesthesia, and about 30 seconds later he sliced the infected cyst open. It hurt like hell, and I let out a little yelp. I don't think the anesthesia had fully kicked in yet.

Margo and the nurse were both standing behind me, watching the doctor work. Right as Dr. Frank made the first cut, I heard both women gasp loudly and jump back. There was so much pressure that the gunk in my cyst had shot several feet in their direction. I turned my head and could see droplets of puss all over the floor, stretching as far as four or five feet from me. Gross.

At least that was all done. Now we could get this thing bandaged up and be on our way. Or so I thought. But instead, Dr. Frank squeezed on the cyst to get it fully drained, and Wow! did that hurt. I'm sure I was making whimpering noises, but Dr. Frank just kept squeezing and squeezing. Finally he finished. As he took off the gloves, he said "You really should try to keep that clean for a few days. I'm not saying you're not clean people, but you should really make an effort." Then he walked out. The whole interaction with him didn't really give me the warm fuzzies, but at least he'd fixed me up.

The nurse bandaged up my back and gave Margo instructions on what to do with me for the next few days. They basically involved squeezing puss out of my back every few hours. She also gave me a prescription for antibiotics, to knock down the infection.

We left the doctor's office and checked into a cheap motel in the middle of town. We planned on staying there for two nights. I could tell that my back was going to need a couple of days to recover before I put my pack on again.

The next morning we popped into the German bakery across the street from our hotel for coffee and a little breakfast. As soon as we sat down at our table,

Tommy walked in the front door.

"Hey, long time no see," he said when he saw us. It had been a week or so since we'd run into him. "How has your hike been going?"

"It's been great," Margo said. "We're still loving it every day. How about you?"

"Same," he replied. "And isn't this a great town? I like how it's small and walkable."

"And great food," I added. "The BBQ place down the block is good, and Margo got a bowl of pho yesterday for the first time on this trip. It's a great town to take a zero. Are you staying here tonight?"

"Yes, I got in last night. I'll take a zero and head out tomorrow. I want to rest my knee for a day, it's giving me a little trouble. What about you guys?

"Same," I said. "We're heading out tomorrow morning."

"Hey, would you guys mind," Tommy asked, "if I stuck with you for a while? I don't want to go through the Sierras alone."

We were about a week away from entering the Sierra Nevada mountain range. It would be the most remote part of the trail. It was also higher in elevation than anything we'd been through so far. It was still pretty early in the season, the third week of May, so that meant that there would be plenty of snow left up there, especially over the higher passes. How to handle this snow had been a major topic of conversation among our fellow hikers for the past week. Was it worth the weight to carry an ice axe? Or would micro-spikes alone be enough traction on the snow? Should we slow down and let the snow melt a little, or just keep pushing on through? The discussions and possible permutations were endless. Our plan was to go without ice axes, and to just push through whatever late spring snow was left, rather than spending time waiting for it to melt. I'd done quite a bit of hiking up in the High Sierra, including some trips around this time of the year, so I was pretty confident that we could handle it.

Regardless of gear choices and timing, the common wisdom among PCT hikers was that it was smart to team up though the mountains. It wasn't somewhere anyone wanted to be all alone. It was a remote and rugged stretch of the trail, and the snow added an extra level of risk. Having someone else to watch your back was safer, and generally the larger the group the better. People who had been hiking alone or with loose groups through the desert were all forming firm, committed groups for the journey through the mountains.

"Of course," I replied to Tommy's request. "The more the merrier." Having an extra person along was good for us, too. "So the knee is still bothering you?" Tommy's knee had started bothering him a hundred miles back or so. Overuse injuries were becoming more and more common and were often a topic of conversation.

"It's OK. It hurts on the downhills, but the uphills are fine. I'm planning to spend the afternoon locked in my hotel room with a bag of ice on it. Hopefully that will help. I really wanted to give my knee a soak in the hot tub at the Acton KOA, but it was closed when I got there."

"Closed?" My eyebrows went up. "That's weird. It was open when we were there. A bunch of us soaked in it. It was like a disgusting lukewarm hiker soup. Hiker soup spiced by hanging blister skin and dirty feet. When were you there?"

"I was there on Wednesday," Tommy replied. We'd been there on Tuesday. "Apparently the health inspector came and closed it down that morning. Unbelievably high levels of bacteria in the water or something."

Two realizations hit me at that moment, neither of them good. First, the big group of hikers in the hot tub on Tuesday with me is at least partially responsible for all that hot tub bacteria, and maybe completely responsible. And second, is it possible the teeming bacteria in that hot tub is what infected my back cyst?

"All right, let's meet up here tomorrow morning at 8am, grab a coffee, and get back to it." Tommy gathered his coat and headed out the door, off to ice his knee for the day. We enjoyed a wonderful day in Tehachapi, eating as much as we could manage, and, most pleasurably, not hiking.

I could see Margo coming up the trail a couple hundred yards behind me, and Tommy another couple hundred yards behind her. From my vantage point on the top of the ridge, I saw the dusty strip of the trail dropping down in front of me through sharp rocks punctuated with cactus and Joshua trees. No doubt it climbed up that steep mountain on the other side of the valley. The sky was blue and cloudless, and the 360-degree view from the ridgeline was breathtaking. Even so, the desert was starting to wear on all of us, with the lack of water, rattlesnakes, and worsening heat. We'd been in it for a month and a half now. We were ready for a major change, and it was coming in the High Sierras.

"Break time?" Margo asked as she crested the ridge.

"Sure," I said. "I could go for a snack."

We found a flat-ish rock to sit on and munched on sesame sticks and almonds.

"How's your back doing?" Margo asked.

"It feels great," I said. Indeed it did. It stung a bit occasionally, and Margo had to change the bandage once a day. But for the most part, it was healing surprisingly quickly.

"Are you still taking the antibiotics?"

"Yes, every day, like clockwork." I really wanted to avoid the hassle of another doctor visit on this hike, so I was doing everything I could to make sure this thing healed properly, including taking the antibiotics with fanatical devotion.

"I'm about tired of the desert," Tommy said, as he joined us at our little seat on the ridge top. "I'm ready to get to some excitement."

"The mountains are going to be so exciting," Margo replied. "I can't wait to get up there. And we're going to be able to quit carrying so much water around. It's everywhere up there!"

"That'll be such a treat after the desert," Tommy said. "Carrying water is such a drag, especially when we have to dry camp. It's going to be so luxurious to just have it everywhere."

"We're just a few days away from getting into the

really high peaks," I added. "I just hope the snow isn't too bad."

"I saw a picture of Forester Pass on Facebook," Tommy said. "It looks a little sketchy."

"Yeah, I saw that too," Margo replied. "I hope we're going to be all right with just spikes. I'm nervous."

Sketchy was right. Forrester pass was the high point of the entire PCT, and there was still a lot of snow on top of it. The part that was concerning us was a chute just below the top that we would have to cross. This early in the season, the chute was still choked with steep, icy snow that we'd have to cross. Based on the pictures we'd seen, it looked like the sort of snow chute where if you fell, it would all be over. The only thing we could do at this point to allay our fears was to talk about the pass, so that's what we did. We talked about it a lot.

"I'm nervous too. We'll just do what we can." I tried to sound reassuring. "If we get into something that any of us thinks isn't safe, we can just turn around. We're all in agreement on that?"

"Sure, I agree," Tommy replied.

"Same," said Margo.

"By the way, is anyone else noticing the sun getting stronger?" I asked. "I don't know if it's the elevation or if it's because we're getting closer to summer, but I'm getting sunburnt on my neck all of a sudden, even with sunscreen on."

"I haven't noticed," Tommy said. I could tell by his tone of voice he thought I may have kicked one too many cactuses on that last climb.

The look Margo gave me made it clear that she hadn't noticed either, and that in fact maybe I should I

Michael Tyler

keep my crazy notions to myself.

The next night, we camped on top of a ridge with a spectacular view of the desert to the east. A steep cliff dropped down a couple thousand feet, giving us wide views of the flat, brown desert floor below, stretching off towards a blue ridgeline of low peaks lining the horizon. It was a warm night, and the three of us were lounging around, finishing up our dehydrated, carb-heavy dinners.

"I don't know what's going on," I complained. "My neck, the back of my hands, they're getting sunburnt so badly. I'm almost out of sunscreen. Today I had to wear a bandanna on my neck all afternoon, it was hurting so bad."

"Weird," Tommy said. "I haven't noticed anything."

"Me neither," chimed in Margo. "I wonder if there's anything else different. Maybe you've got a bad batch of sunscreen."

"Maybe," I replied, though I'd been using the same sunscreen for a couple hundred miles with no problems. I had to figure out some way of dealing with this. The weather forecast was typical for the desert — nothing but sunshine and blue skies for the foreseeable future.

"Antibiotics!" Margo suddenly exclaimed. "Don't some antibiotics increase your sensitivity to the sun?"

"Hey, that sounds right," I said, vaguely remembering hearing something like that somewhere. I fumbled through my pack for the bottle of antibiotics I'd been taking so religiously. Sure enough, the label had a warning to limit exposure to sunlight while taking them.

"Well, now I don't know what to do. I've got to keep taking these. I really don't want that infection to come back. But this is pretty much the worst time to be sun-sensitive. We're in the desert. I don't think we've seen even a single cloud in two days. It's going to be nothing but sun."

"I have some gloves," Tommy offered. The backs of my hands were where I was getting burnt the worst. "Why don't you wear them while you're on the antibiotics?"

"Great, thanks Tommy," I said. "If I wear those, and keep the bandanna over my neck, maybe I'll make it to Kennedy Meadows. I can definitely get some sunscreen there."

"Sure thing," said Tommy. "Whatever I can do to help. Now I'm off to bed. It's 8:30, after all."

Margo and I sat out in the warm desert evening a few minutes longer, watching the ridgeline across the valley change colors slowly, almost imperceptibly. First brown, then orange as the setting sun reflected off them. Then blue as the first stars appeared in the sky above us. And finally black, as night enveloped the California desert. As usual, the stars shone brightly, unimpeded by clouds and undimmed by any city lights. The air felt warm, without the chill that had crept in at night earlier in the spring. It was a beautiful evening in the southern California desert.

"What's your plan for the mountains?" I asked. I

was sitting at a table in Grumpy Bears, one of two restaurants in the tiny town of Kennedy Meadows. A soft spoken Canadian couple that we'd just met, Mars and Coyote, shared my table, along with our hiking partner Tommy.

Kennedy Meadows is the official jumping off point for the High Sierra. It's the last town that the trail passes anywhere near for the next 300 miles. It's not even much of a town, to be honest. There are a couple of restaurants, both with just the basics on the menu. There is a small outfitter that helps PCT hikers resupply and carries some necessary gear, but that was about it. Margo was over at the outfitter store now, getting gear to get her through the upcoming snow.

"We're tired of all the fear mongering. We're just going to go," Mars replied. Mars and Coyote had hiked the Appalachian Trail together a couple of years earlier and had learned to ignore the constant hiker chatter on that trip. It was a good lesson, and they were applying it now.

"Lots of people are killing time here," Coyote added. She was finishing off the biggest pancake I'd ever seen, larger than a dinner plate and a solid inch thick. Grumpy Bears offered all you can eat pancakes with their breakfasts, which speaks directly to PCT hikers' hearts and stomachs. But realistically, even the hungriest among us couldn't eat more than one of these monstrosities.

"I was talking to a group yesterday who had been here five days already," she continued, "and they still don't know when they're going to leave."

"I think we're just going to go too," I said. "I can't

imagine hanging out here for more than a day or two. I'd go stir crazy sitting around this restaurant all day. And I don't think the snow up in the mountains is that bad anyway. I'm sure we'll be all right."

"So, what's the plan for the Sierras once we get up there?" Tommy asked. "What are we thinking in terms of miles per day and stuff like that?"

Having lived in California for the previous 20 years, I'd spent lots of time in the High Sierra, and I knew it well. This was the part of the trail I was most excited about, and I had a plan for how to go about getting through all the snow that was still up there.

"The trail through the mountains is a series of passes separated by deep valleys," I said. "Every day, we'll go over a pass, hike down into a valley, and then climb up towards the next pass." I grabbed a napkin off a table and drew a rudimentary map, a line representing the trail bisected by a six or eight other lines representing passes. "See, here we go over Forrester pass, then we head down here, into the valley, and get as close as we can to the next pass, Glenn. These passes will all be covered with snow, so we should try to go over them in the morning when the snow is still frozen solid. If the snow gets soft, it'll just get slippery, and our micro-spikes won't work. And if it gets really soft, like maybe after noon, we'll start to post-hole, or fall in to the snow up to our knees, or maybe our even our hips. Post-holing is no fun, and even a little dangerous since you never know what's underneath the snow."

"I see," Tommy replied. "So we cross the pass first thing in the morning, then get as close as we can to the next pass in the afternoon, camp, and cross then next one early the next day. Then repeat."

"Exactly," I said. "And repeat, and repeat, and repeat. The passes are all just about a day apart. Really, most are like twelve to fifteen miles apart, so we'll have some short days. But that's the way to do this. Doing two passes in a day would be tough, plus we'd have to do one in the late afternoon, which would make it extra challenging."

"That sounds about like our plan," Mars said. He and Coyote had been sitting there watching the whole exposition. "That definitely seems like the best way to handle the snow."

Just then Margo walked into the restaurant, looking dejected. "No micro-spikes," she said. "They don't carry them." I'd mailed micro-spikes to myself in the resupply package we'd picked up here at Kennedy Meadows, but Margo had planned on buying them here. There was only one outfitter in town, and apparently they had some sort of moral opposition to micro-spikes. So we were stuck.

"We can't go through the mountains without spikes," I said. Word on the trail was that even going with spikes was risky. Some people were still heading out fully equipped with crampons and ice axes. Micro-spikes were the bare minimum equipment we'd need. Without them, there was no way we could leave Kennedy Meadows and go into the mountains.

"We could order them on Amazon and get them shipped here," Margo suggested. "It'll take a couple of days, but I guess that's more time for the snow to melt."

"I guess," I said. I really didn't want to hang out in this tiny town, killing time while we waited for the UPS truck. But it didn't seem that we had any choice.

"It's fine with me," Tommy chimed in. "My knee could really use a few days off."

"What's up with your knee?" asked Coyote.

"It's an overuse thing," Tommy explained, "and it's been getting worse. Usually it really hurts on the downhills, and for the last couple of days it's been hurting on the uphills too. It's starting to really slow me down. Hopefully a couple of days of rest will help it."

"I hope so," I say. "Think of all the people who have already dropped out because of overuse injuries. I'd say it's like one out of every five people we started with. This trail is tough on the body. I the rest does you some good."

"Me too," Tommy said quietly. His dejected expression didn't broadcast confidence. "How is your knee holding up, by the way?"

"It's great," I replied. I was still wearing the knee brace every day, so everyone I met could immediately tell something was going on with my knee. "It's actually not even painful anymore. I keep wearing the brace, mostly out of superstition. Like if I quit wearing it and then hurt myself, I'll feel silly. But there's no pain now. It looks like, for me at least, hiking is the best medicine."

"I wish it was working for me," Tommy replied.

"Did you have any luck finding sunscreen?" Margo asked. I was still getting sunburnt every day, and I had 3 days of antibiotics left to take. I looked ridiculous on the trail now, with every square centimeter of skin that I could possibly cover swathed in some kind of clothing. I wore gloves and long sleeves even on the hottest days, a bandanna stuck in my hat so that it hung down over my neck like a miniature cape, and my ball cap pulled down as close to my eyes as I could manage. And still I'd get sunburned.

"Yes, I scored big time in the hiker box. I found these." I held up my sunscreen booty. There were no full bottles of sunscreen in the hiker box, but there were 2 nearly empty bottles, which would carry me until the antibiotics ran out, and a roll-on 50 SPF sunscreen stick that looked like it would protect the most exposed spots. "I think this will cover me."

"That's great. It looks like we're all ready to go into the mountains," Margo said, "except for my micro-spikes. I guess we should place the order. There's really nothing else we can do."

The UPS truck arrived in the afternoon two days later. We were so ready to leave. We'd been ready to leave for two days. Despite the constant fear mongering about snow levels, we were bored with Kennedy Meadows and eager to get up into the "real mountains". Ten minutes after the UPS truck drove away, we were hiking out.

We were brimming with anticipation. Though it would be a few days before we got up into the highest of the Sierras, it felt great to be done with the desert and heading on to a new phase of this adventure. We felt like we were ready for anything.

Part 2: The Sierra

Chapter 4: Wild Mountains

The first couple of days out of Kennedy Meadows were a bit of a let down. Even though Kennedy Meadows is officially the end of the desert, Mother Nature didn't get the memo. We would occasionally walk alongside the Kern River, which was without a doubt the biggest river we'd seen on the hike so far. Having access to such abundant water felt luxurious. But otherwise, the scenery was similar to what we'd been hiking through since Tehachapi. We were still surrounded by low desert scrub, punctuated by occasional, widely spaced trees. The hills to the east and west were starting to rise up into something that looked more like mountains, but it was happening slowly.

Tommy wasn't impressed. "The Sierras are off to a disappointing start," Tommy said in camp on our second night out of Kennedy Meadows.

"Yeah," Margo agreed. "It looks a lot like the desert here."

"How's your knee doing?" Margo asked Tommy. He'd been behind us all day, trying to nurse his knee as much as possible.

"OK," Tommy replied. "That rest in Kennedy Meadows helped, but it's still pretty painful. How's your sunburn doing, Mike?"

"Better," I said. I still had one day left on the antibiotics, so I'd been layering on the sunscreen. "This little roll-on tube of sunscreen is helping a lot on my hands." I held up my hands to illustrate. It was a poor illustration. They were still pretty red, and in fact they looked like they might even be a little swollen.

"That doesn't look great," Tommy said. "You should keep wearing my gloves for a while."

"It's so hot," I replied. "My hands sweat too much. I'll just keep layering on this 50 SPF stuff. That'll protect me."

As we got ready for bed that night, Margo said, "I'm going to do a little experiment as we hike through the Sierras. Every night, I'm going to put a couple of sticks on top of our bear canisters. I want to see if anything ever messes with them."

In the Sierras, the National Park Service and the National Forests require everyone to store all their food in a bear canister, which is a small, lightweight plastic barrel. Bears can be incredibly creative when it comes to getting food, and bear canisters are a foolproof way to keep food safe. There had been a lot of talk about bears as we got closer to the Sierras. Most people wanted to see a bear, but no one wanted to get too close to one, or to lose their food to one while they slept. Margo's experiment would be a good way to get a sense for how often bears are actually sniffing around camp.

"That sounds like a great plan," I replied. "Surely at least one bear will sniff our food somewhere in these mountains."

The next morning at breakfast, Margo eyed my hand as I spooned oatmeal into my mouth. "That sunburn on your hand got worse overnight. How is that possible?"

"Yeah," I said. "And look. There are some blisters popping up." On each hand, there were a couple of little blisters just starting to appear. "Maybe I'll wear your gloves today after all, Tommy. Hey, did anything knock the sticks off your bear can last night?"

"Nope," replied Margo, clearly a little disappointed. "It was just like I'd left it."

That night we camped in a wide flat spot right next to a little burbling stream that came down out of the mountains rising off to the west. Wildflowers accented the otherwise monochromatic green scrub brush that surrounded us on all sides. To the east and west, high ridges spiked with granite peaks rose up out of the wide, flat valley floor. We set up our tents and gathered together for dinner on the bank of the little stream.

"I've never been sunburned like this," I complained as I waited for a pot of water to come to a boil. "Both my hands are swollen like balloons." I held up both my hands with my palms facing towards me. My hands were so swollen you could barely see knuckles beneath the bulging skin. The blisters had increased in both size and number since that morning as well. My hands looked terrible. "At least my antibiotics are gone. Hopefully I'll get some of my natural sun protection back soon."

95

"That looks like more than a sunburn." Tommy looked concerned. "I think you're having a reaction to something."

"Yeah," Margo agreed. "It looks like a poison ivy reaction."

"I haven't seen any poison oak in days," I said. But Margo was right, this didn't look like a run-of-the-mill sunburn. "But even if it is, what can we do? We're in the middle of nowhere here. Even if I wanted to see a doctor, I'm not sure where I'd go. Probably to Lone Pine, I guess." Lone Pine was off the trail, but it was also still several days north of us.

"I guess there's nothing we can do but keep walking," Margo replied. That was really our only choice.

We continued north the next morning, and over the course of the day my hands got worse and worse. They continued to swell, and a wicked rash developed on both hands.

"I have a theory," I said during a lunch break the next day. "I think that someone rubbed this sunscreen stick I've been using on themselves after they'd touched some poodle dog bush. Somehow the poodle dog bush oil got all over the stick, and then they unwittingly left it in the hiker box at Kennedy Meadows."

Poodle dog bush is a plant that in recent years has surged in southern California, especially in areas that have recently burned in a wildfire. Like poison oak, it contains a toxin that generates an allergic reaction in most people. I knew I was sensitive to poison oak. I'd never touched a poodle dog bush plant before, but it looked like I was pretty sensitive to that as well.

"That sounds like a pretty good guess," Margo replied. "I can't think of any other explanation for what's going on with your hands."

"Great," I moaned. "I made it all the way through the desert successfully dodging poison oak and poodle dog bush, and then I get it from a hiker box?"

"I wonder how long the reaction will last", Tommy said.

"I don't know," I replied, "but I hope it gets better soon. It's painful."

About three days later, the swelling started going down, and the redness started to fade. It had been nearly a month since I soaked in the hot tub at the Acton KOA. That soak had led to the infected cyst on my back, which had led to countless antibiotic induced sunburns, which had in turn led to a poodle dog bush reaction. I remember that hot tub soak felt great, but there's no way it felt THAT great. I hoped I had finally reached the end of that chain reaction.

A couple evenings later, Margo and I were camped alone next to a little burbling stream named Diaz Creek. Our campsite was in a little stand of trees, with the creek about 100 yards away. It had continued to be pretty dry since we left Kennedy Meadows, but tomorrow we would enter the real High Sierras. We hadn't seen Tommy since we left camp that morning. He'd been nursing his knee, taking it really slow to prepare for the high passes that were just ahead.

As we were finishing dinner, Tommy came limping

into camp. He was clearly exhausted and looked to be in a fair amount of pain as well.

"How's the knee?" I asked, as he walked towards us. Based on the way he was favoring his left leg, I already had a pretty good idea how he would answer.

"Not good," Tommy said, looking dejected. "Now it has started hurting when I go up, and it's constant agony on the descents. It's getting worse every day."

"Oh, man. I'm so sorry," I replied. I knew knee pain well, and Tommy had my deepest sympathies.

"I think I'm going to have to bail out at Lone Pine."

"What?!? Are you sure?"

"I've thought a lot about this," Tommy said. "I really don't see any other way." This was a huge deal. Tommy had come over from Europe to do this hike, had arranged everything in his life so that he could put it on hold for 5 months. Leaving the trail after only a month and a half had to be devastating.

We spent the next hour talking through his strategy and plans. He'd go down to Lone Pine and wait in a hotel for a couple of days to feel things out. He would rest his knee, and ice it as much as he could over those few days. If it felt better, he could ease back into the hike, taking it slow to begin with. But he wasn't optimistic. If, after a couple days, he didn't feel significant improvement, he would have to book a ticket back to Denmark and figure out how to spend the rest of the summer.

It was a very demoralizing evening. We were on the cusp of entering the High Sierra, widely regarded as the best section of the trail. It was a stretch of the trail that we had all talked about and eagerly anticipated since the start of the hike. Now Tommy would have to bail out just before it began. What's more, we'd really enjoyed hiking and spending time with him, and it was going to be sad to see him go. It was also a reminder that any of us could go down on this hike, at any time. It would take a lot of luck to stay healthy all the way to Canada. We went to bed feeling a little morose that evening.

We would part ways the next day when Tommy headed down into Lone Pine to rest. We were rooting for him; we knew what a big deal it was for him to continue on with the hike. But his knee didn't improve in Lone Pine, and he wound up going back to Denmark a few days later. We never saw Tommy again.

"I see a spot over there," Margo indicated a flat spot underneath a small grove of trees, across a green meadow dotted with tents and hikers soaking in the warm afternoon sun.

"That looks good from here," I replied. "Let's check it out."

We were at Crabtree Meadows, looking for a spot to camp for the next two nights. It was our second full day in the High Sierras, and so far the mountains were living up to their billing. There was water everywhere. After having to carry liters — and sometimes gallons — of water in the desert, we now sometimes walked all day without carrying a drop of water. We would drink from streams as we passed them, comfortable knowing that if we got thirsty we'd pass the next stream soon. It felt absolutely luxurious.

The scenery in the High Sierra didn't disappoint. We had been talking about and anticipating being in this sublime wilderness for over six weeks now, so it would have been easy to build up unrealistic expectations. But as high as our expectations were, the Sierras were delivering. Lush valleys were filled with sparkling lakes, burbling streams, and carpeted with pine trees. The valleys were ringed by sharp granite peaks, some bare, some still holding the late spring snow. The barren, exposed granite peaks offered a sharp contrast to the lushness of the valleys they encompassed. It was exactly the paradise we'd been anticipating throughout the desert, and no one was the least bit disappointed with it.

"This looks good to me," Margo said, walking around our potential campsite. "Nice and flat, and kind of away from everyone. I can't believe how crowded it is here." There must have been 40 tents spread across the large meadow, along with lots of happy hikers lounging in the sun and going about camp chores.

"Everyone wants to summit Whitney," I said, stating the obvious.

Mt. Whitney is the highest peak in the continental US, at 14,500 feet above sea level. Mt. Whitney is not actually on the PCT, but it's close. The PCT passes about 8 miles to the west of the summit. Most PCT hikers can't pass up the opportunity to bag the highest peak in the continental US as part of their thru hike. After all, it's so close, everyone is already well acclimated to the elevation, and in we're all in excellent shape by now. It was an easy and worthwhile detour.

Crabtree Meadows is the last good, legal campsite before the summit, so virtually every PCT hiker spends at least one night here. Most people spend the night before waking up very early and heading up to summit. Many people will also spend a second night after they summit, heading on towards Forrester pass the following day. That was our plan.

"I hope it's not too icy up there," Margo said, gazing to the east towards Mt. Whitney.

"Yeah, me too," I replied. "Maybe we can find someone who went up today and they can give us some info."

"Hey guys," Yoda said as he walked up. Right on cue.

"Hey Yoda," I said. "Long time no see." We had met Yoda about halfway through the desert and had been on roughly the same schedule as him for the last 300 miles or so. He was a wilderness guide in the Utah desert, and he had some great stories. Margo and I got along very well with him from the time we met him. We hadn't seen him in the previous week as he had been a little ahead of us while we messed around in Tehachapi. "Did you go up Whitney today?"

"Yep," he replied. "I got up to the summit around 10am. It was clear and calm up there, really pretty warm. And the views from up there are amazing!"

"Was there much snow on the way up?" I asked.

"A couple of patches, but nothing serious. Maybe one or two places where you might want an ice axe, but you'll be fine with just micro-spikes."

"Great, thanks for the info. Looks like it's on for tomorrow, then," I said, turning towards Margo.

"Yes, it's on," she replied excitedly. I'd been up on top of Mt. Whitney during some of my previous Sierra escapades, but it would be Margo's first time. Naturally, she was excited.

"How are guys liking the mountains so far?" Yoda asked.

"They're great!" Margo replied enthusiastically. We were only a couple of days into the High Sierra, but we're loving it so far. "I love the views, and having water everywhere is wonderful!"

"I'm loving them too," I added. "I really think this is going to be the best part of the whole trip, so I really want to savor it up here."

"It's gorgeous up here, I have to agree," Yoda said. "I'm going to try to savor it too. But I also don't want to run out of food, so I don't want to slow down too much. I guess we've just got to find the right balance."

"I'm just worried that when we're done with these mountains, we're not going to have anything to look forward to," I said. "We won't even be halfway done with the trail, but the best part will be behind us."

"Oh, come on," Yoda replied. "How can you know that? Enjoy the mountains as we go through them, but I don't think we can predict where the highlights are going to be already. We've still got a long summer ahead of us."

"Yeah," Margo piled on. "Enjoy the hike as it comes. Just enjoy living in the moment."

I grumbled something under my breath. I'd hiked this part of the trail before, and I knew it was going to be beautiful. Who were these people to tell me to adjust my expectations?

After an early dinner, we climbed into our sleeping bags while the sun still shone down on the meadow. We were planning an early start tomorrow.

My phone chirped annoyingly at 4:30 am. It was still dark outside, and bitterly cold. We ate some oatmeal silently in the dark, and by 5am we were hiking out of camp, just as the predawn light illuminated the meadow. Since most of the other PCT hikers had got an even earlier start to make the summit for sunrise, we had the trail to ourselves.

An hour later we hit the first snow we'd seen in the Sierras, and in fact the first we'd seen since we were caught in the storm just outside of Idyllwild. It was a patch of snow left over from the winter, frozen solid and covering the trail. There was no way around it.

"Should we put on our spikes?" Margo inquired.

"Yeah, it seems like it's time."

It took us a few minutes to get them on. Eventually we would put them on what seemed like a hundred times as we went through these mountains. Eventually we would get a lot better at putting them on and taking them off, but this first time took some concentration.

"Just be careful here," I said, stepping out onto the icy snow. "A slip here could be bad news."

"No kidding," Margo said, following the snow chute down with her eyes. The icy snowfield ended abruptly in a sea of sharp rocks about 100 feet below us. If you fell here, there would be no way to stop yourself without an ice axe, until you hit those sharp rocks. They'd end your slide, and it wouldn't be a soft landing.

We gingerly crossed the icy patch and continued on

up towards the summit. The micro-spikes worked great on that patch, and on the rest of the snow we encountered on the way up. It reassured us that maybe we had the right snow gear for all of the upcoming high passes as well.

Around 11am, we reached the summit. "Congratulations!" I high fived Margo as she crested the final rise and stood on the summit for the first time. "High point of the continental US." We were both sporting broad grins.

Yoda was right; the view up here was spectacular. To the east, the mountain dropped off quickly down to the Owens valley, 10,000 feet below us. The flat desert of the valley floor stretched as far as the eye could see north and south. To the east, across the Owens valley, White Mountains rose up out of the desert to peaks that appeared to be just as high as the one we were standing on. A touch of snow still covered the highest peaks over there.

In every other direction, to the south, north, and especially west, the snow-covered, jagged peaks of the Sierras filled our view. It looked like an endless landscape of snowy mountains. Looking to the north, we could see many other high peaks that we'd pass by over the next couple of weeks. It was an awe-inspiring view.

The sun was out, and the air was warm with barely a breeze in the air. We spent an hour on the summit, soaking in the views and savoring a lunch of — what else? — peanut butter and tortillas.

"I have to say, this is about as good as it gets." I was very content. "Not just summiting this mountain, but having the chance to live this thru hiking lifestyle. We're outside every day. We wake up in a beautiful place, spend all day walking through beautiful landscapes, and then camp in a beautiful spot. We're surrounded by nature all day, every day. I can't imagine a better way to spend time."

"Yeah," Margo agreed. "I feel happier and more at peace than I can ever remember feeling."

"What are we going to do when this is over, and we can't live like this anymore?" I wondered aloud.

"Don't worry sweetie," Margo replied. "We've still got 1800 miles to go. This is going to go on forever."

Of course we both knew it wouldn't. But on that summit, on that gorgeous late spring morning, it was easy to pretend it would.

"I hope it doesn't get too cold up here," Margo said, as we finished laying out our sleeping bags inside our tent.

"It sure looks barren, "I replied, scanning the plateau. "It'll be chilly, but as long as the wind doesn't pick up tonight, I think we'll be all right."

We had set up camp on a barren plateau at about 12,000 feet above sea level. No trees can survive up here, just some short, scrubby grasses punctuated by tiny red, white and purple wildflowers. Large patches of late spring snow still covered much of the plateau, and a stream ran down in a gully right below our campsite. Sheer granite walls rose up on three sides of us, with the valley dropping off steeply to the south, the direction we'd come. Up ahead in the distance a sheer granite wall loomed above us. At the top of this wall was Forrester pass, the high point on the PCT.

This is the pass that everyone had been talking about for the last several hundred miles. It's the first high pass that the PCT crosses. It's also the highest point on the entire PCT, over 13,000 feet above sea level. Since it's up so high, the snow sticks around until late in the hiking season. There's a chute on the south side — the side we would go up — that was everyone's top concern. We'd seen pictures on Facebook, and it looked frightening. It was a steep chute that was choked with a wide tongue of snow. The snow tongue was long enough that there was no way to go above or below it. We'd have to cross it. Without an ice axe, if we lost our footing while we were crossing it there would be no stopping a fall. Since we'd decided not to carry ice axes in order to keep our packs a little lighter, our strategy on this pass was simple. Don't fall.

"You can see the pass right there," I said, pointing at a little notch in the soaring granite in front of us that was just barely visible. "And just below it, there's the snow chute we've got to cross. It doesn't look so bad from down here."

"I don't know," Margo replied. "That looks like a long way up to me."

Just then, Mars and Coyote came walking across the trail towards our camp.

"Hey guys," Margo waved at them as they approached. "See Forrester up there?" She pointed to the little notch in the ridgeline.

"Is that it?" Mars asked, eyeing the wall. "That's way

up there."

"I'm pretty sure that's it," I said. "I hope that snow chute's not too sketchy."

"Same here," Mars replied.

"Where are you guys heading for tonight?" I asked.

"It looks like there's one more stream about half a mile ahead, so we'll camp there. We're going to head out super early tomorrow to hit the snow when it's still frozen. What about you guys?"

"We're planning on starting around 5am, I think," I replied. "We really want to be off the other side before the snow gets soft." Everyone had the same basic strategy for going over these passes — go over early in the morning and be on the other side and off the snow before the mid-day warming set in.

"We'll probably see you up there somewhere," Mars said, as they hoisted their packs. "Enjoy your night up here."

"Thanks," I replied. "You guys too. Stay warm. We'll see you tomorrow."

"Well, this is definitely it," I said, looking across the snow field in front of me. "I recognize it from the Facebook pictures."

"It's not that far across. Just don't look down," Mars said. We'd met up with Mars and Coyote just as we started the straight-up-the-wall part of the hike, and we had all stuck together for the climb up to the snow chute. Maybe we could get one of them to be our guinea pig, to go across the sketchy snowfield first.

"Yeah, that's a steep drop," I replied. The snow chute was maybe 50 yards wide. It wouldn't take too many steps to cross it. But the chute was steep. The snow tongue continued down for about 200 feet below the point where the trail crossed it, and ended in a jumble of sharp rocks. Without ice axes, we wouldn't be able to stop ourselves if we fell on the slick, steep snow. We'd slide down to the end of the snow and then hit those sharp rocks. No one had to say it, but it was obvious that a fall here would be very bad. Like 'you could die' kind of bad.

"Let's just go across one at a time," Margo suggested. "Slow and easy."

"Yes, slow and easy," I agreed. "I'll go first." So much for guinea pigs.

I took my first step on the chute. The snow was frozen solid. "My micro-spikes are gripping it. They're gripping it really well. " My footing felt very secure. I tried not to think about the icy chute plummeting down just below my left foot.

I stuck my hiking pole into the frozen snow and picked up my right foot. I planted it down a foot in front of me, making sure the spikes gripped the snow well. Then I picked up my left foot and moved it forward, again making sure it was planted as securely as possible. Each foot placement was important. If one foot wasn't secure, when I took a step and picked up the other foot, well… things would turn out badly.

I repeated the procedure across the chute, one step at a time. Step, plant foot, plant pole, step. Over and over. My concentration was intense. Nothing mattered other than my feet and the ice below them. I was 100% in the moment.

Crossing the chute only took a couple of minutes, but while it was happening, it felt like it took forever. When I reached the other side, I turned to see Margo, Mars and Coyote back on the other side, watching me intently.

"It's not as bad as it looks," I yelled back across the chute. "Just focus on where you put your feet. And don't fall."

Margo started across next, and took the same slow, careful approach to crossing. I could tell that the rest of the world faded from her consciousness, just like it had for me. She was focused on her feet and the ice; at that moment, there was nothing else for her. Finally, she also made it across safely.

Mars and then Coyote followed in the same manner. Once we were all across the chute, it was a quick 10 minute climb up a mostly snow free trail to the top of Forrester pass. We were up on top by 7am, at the high point of the PCT.

We were all elated. All of us had been dreading this pass. Since it was the first of the high passes, it was one everyone had been focused on. We had studied pictures of the snow chute online and talked endlessly about how to cross it. Now, that was all behind us. We had made it to the top of our first major pass.

"What an amazing view!" Margo exclaimed as she crested the ridge. From here, the views were spectacular. Looking back to the south, we could see everything we'd walked over the previous day, as well as Mt Whitney off in the distance. The trail wound down across the plateau and into the tree-filled valley beyond it. Looking north, we could see a whole new world that we would hike through over the next few days. Snow-covered peaks ringed the basin in front of us. From here we could see several big, crystalline lakes reflecting the early morning sun. It looked like a mountain wonderland.

"It looks like we've got more snow to go through," Coyote said as she came up to the pass and looked north. Snow still covered a good piece of the north face of the pass, so we'd have an hour or maybe two of hiking through snow on the way down.

"Yeah, we shouldn't mess around up here too long," Margo suggested. "We want to be off that snow before we start post-holing."

"OK, a quick snack and then we go," I replied. "Congratulations on making it to the PCT high point!"

We all exchanged high fives, snapped a bunch of pictures, and headed off into that beautiful mountain wonderland that awaited us to the north.

"This is as far as we can go today," I said as we came up to a flat spot near a river, once again high up on a plateau, above tree line. It was 3pm, 3 or 4 hours before our normal stopping time. "This is the last water before the pass."

"OK, then this is it," Margo agreed. We'd gone over Forrester pass early that morning. Glen pass was only 12 trail miles from Forrester pass. Even though we were averaging 20 miles a day going through the desert, the terrain in the Sierra was forcing us to slow down. We really didn't want to go over Glen pass in the afternoon.

We had heard that there was still quite a bit of snow up on top of the pass, and neither of us wanted to spend the afternoon post-holing in the soft snow. We'd follow a similar pattern for the next week: climb up over a high pass first thing in the morning, then hike to the base of the next pass, camping as close to the pass as we could get without sleeping on the snow.

"It's going to be cold up here again tonight," Margo said worriedly. We were up above 11,000 feet, not quite as high as the previous night, but still high enough that we would probably wake up with ice in our water bottles.

We got our camp set up and settled in for a relaxing late afternoon. We didn't stop early very often, so we savored it when we did. The sun was still beating down on our campsite, keeping us warm. Since we had hit the mountains, we had noticed that as soon as the sun goes behind the ridge in the evening, the warmth goes away almost instantly. So it was nice to savor some sunny moments while relaxing at camp. I pulled my Kindle out of my pack and found a nice rock that would work as a back rest. It felt unbelievably good to just relax in the mountains.

After half an hour, Mars and Coyote came along. "Hey guys, is this the last water?" Coyote asked.

"I think so," I said. "Are you guys stopping here?"

"Yep. We heard Glen pass is a little sketchy, and we don't want to go over it in the late afternoon."

We spent the evening with Mars and Coyote swapping stories from the trail, and trading gossip about other hikers we'd met along the way. Mars and Coyote were full of wild stories from their Applachian Trail hike the previous year.

"What time are you guys heading out tomorrow?" I asked as the sun got lower in the sky. It was just after 8pm, and even with the sun still just above the horizon the temperature was dropping. Everyone was thinking about how nice their warm sleeping bag was going to feel.

"I think 5am," Mars said. "That worked well for us this morning on Forrester."

"Yeah, same here," I replied. "We'll see you guys in the morning."

The next morning we once again rolled out of bed in the predawn chill. Margo and I each choked down a protein bar for breakfast, and by 5am we were all ready to conquer Glen pass.

Going up towards the pass wasn't bad. The south side barely had any snow, and we wondered about all the warnings we had heard about Glenn pass. But once we hit the pass and got a view of the north side, we saw how much everything was about to change.

"Wow, that is a LOT of snow," Margo said as she reached the pass and surveyed the white blanket to the north. On top of the pass we had a brand new view of a whole new basin. The slope going down off the north side of the pass was completely covered in deep snow, without much of a consistent track across it. Footsteps wound down in multiple paths across the snowfield. In the basin far below us was Rae Lakes, one of the most renowned of the remote lakes on the High Sierra. The lakes were beautiful, filling the bottom of the basin. Snow lined slopes with sharp granite peaks shot up around the lakes on all sides.

"Yeah, it's a ton of snow. And it's pretty steep. I see why people are saying this is sketchy."

Leaving the pass, we first had to cross the top of a big bowl, traversing right along the upper edge of a steep slope for several hundred yards. A fall here probably wouldn't be fatal, but it was a long way down. It would definitely hurt, and it probably would have ended our trip.

"Watch it going across here," I said as I started off across the top of the bowl. "One step at a time."

"I'm right behind you," Margo said, carefully stepping in my tracks in the snow.

"I wish we had ice axes here," I said. Our micro-spikes were gripping the snow well, but I really, really didn't want to fall.

"Shut up and let me focus," Margo replied. That seemed like smart advice.

As we headed towards the High Sierra, all the talk had been about Forester Pass and how to get over it. I had assumed that was because it was the hardest of the passes we would have to cross. After all, Forrester was the highest, so it must be the most snow choked, right? Wrong. This pass was definitely a more dangerous pass. The chute we had crossed on Forrester was only about 50 feet across. Here we were walking atop an exposed slope for what felt like ten times that far, and then descending through steep snow all the way down to the lakes, easily a thousand feet below us.

We made our way across the top of the bowl step by

step, nervous the whole way. After the bowl, we started the steep descent down the huge snow field towards the lakes. Again, we took it slowly, step by step.

Finally, around 11am, 6 hours after leaving camp, we made it to the end of the snow and down to Rae Lakes.

"Whew, that was harrowing," Margo said as she caught up to me. I was sitting on the edge of the snowfield, taking off my micro-spikes. The trail stretching out in front of me was a muddy mess, but at least it wasn't covered in snow. We were done with the snow, at least for today.

"Yeah," I agreed. "That was way worse than Forester Pass. See that spot down by the lake?" I pointed towards a lovely spot beneath a tree on the lake shore a few hundred feet below us. "Let's get down there and take a nice, long lunch break."

We enjoyed our standard lunch of peanut butter and tortillas on the shore of the beautiful lake. We took off our shoes, completely soaked from a morning of walking through wet snow, and let them and our feet dry in the mid-day sun.

"How many tortillas do we have left?" I asked.

"Looks like 6 more between us." That was one each for lunch for the next 3 days.

"Uh oh. We have 5 days to get to VVR." Vermillion Valley Resort (VVR) was the next place where we could resupply without taking a huge detour off the trail. We had mailed a box of food there when we were down in Bishop several days earlier, so it would be waiting for us there. But it was going to take us a solid 5 days more to get to it, and it looked like we were going to wind up cutting it really close on food.

"I'm getting pretty low on hiking snacks too," Margo said. "How about you?"

"I'm in the same boat," I replied. "We're going to have to be careful with our food. I think we're going to be hungry by the time we get to VVR."

"We've got enough dinners and breakfasts, right?" Margo asked. "We just won't have anything to eat during the day in a few more days. That's going to be miserable, but we'll survive."

"Hey, I have an idea," I offered. "You know those bear boxes that are at some campsites?" At popular campsites in these mountains, the National Park Service puts big, metal boxes with latches where people can store food. The sturdy metal boxes have complicated latches that bears can't figure out, so food is safe inside. Backpackers can store their food in the bins overnight without worrying about rogue bears rifling through it.

"Yeah," Margo replied.

"Well, sometimes I've seen old food that people have left behind in those boxes. Let's check them when we pass by and see if we can find anything edible. Anything we can find is going to help."

"Wait, so you're suggesting eating other people's garbage?" Margo asked.

"Well, technically it's not garbage…" I started, trying to form a defense of my plan that was, when you boiled it down, eating other people's garbage.

"That sounds like a great plan," Margo replied, smiling at me. Wow. I had suggested eating out of the garbage for the next week, and Margo had called that a "great plan". This woman was truly the love of my life.

After we finished eating, we spent some time poking

around on Guthooks and figured out where we would pass bear boxes between here and VVR. We found three along the trail. They were spaced out about a day apart, so we would pass by one per day for the next 3 days. We also did an inventory of the food we had left.

"I've got enough oatmeal and coffee to get through to VVR," I said, "and I have enough dinners too if I can get by on one Top Ramen for the last night. What about you?"

"I'm about the same," Margo told me, looking a little grim. "I'll be OK for breakfast and dinner, but I think I'm going to be out of snack food in a couple of days."

"This is going to be tough. Going through these mountains, up and down over these passes, we're going to be burning tons of calories. Doing it on just a small breakfast and dinner won't be easy."

"Well, we don't have a choice, right?" Margo asked.

"We could hike out at Bishop pass and resupply," I offered, knowing that this probably wasn't a great choice. It would be 12 miles one way just to get to the trailhead at Bishop pass, plus a long, hard hitch down into town. Then, of course, we'd have to hike that 12 miles again to back onto the trail. The extra 24 miles of hiking, plus time to hitch hike into town and resupply, would probably cost us a couple of days.

"Let's just try to push through," Margo suggested. "Maybe the bear boxes will hold some treasure for us along the way." I hoped so. If they didn't, it was going to be a miserable few days.

The next day, right after lunch, we passed by the first of the bear boxes. I walked up to it, knowing that there was a pretty slim chance it would hold anything edible this early in the season.

But lo and behold, when I popped open the bear box, there was food! "Jackpot!" I yelled, as Margo came up the trail to see me with my head stuck inside the bear box as I rummaged.

It wasn't a lot of food. There was a Knorr side (basically a flavored rice packet), a couple of Clif bars, and 3 instant oatmeal packets. It wasn't much, but it was some extra calories, and it looked like we were going to need all we could get.

"What's in there?" Margo asked.

I told her what I'd found. "It's not a lot, but it'll help," I tried to sound optimistic.

"Every little bit helps," she said. Even though we'd just had our meager lunch of a single tortilla with some peanut butter (already we were limiting what we ate, trying to conserve our snacks), we each ate one of the Clif bars on the spot. It helped, but we were both still starving.

The next day, we ate the last of our snack food. We were down to one more lunch each, plus a meager dinner and breakfast for every day we had left to get to VVR. That wasn't a lot of food under any circumstances, and since we were hiking ten or twelve hours a day it was woefully inadequate. We were both hungry constantly, and we talked nonstop about food. We talked about what we'd eat when we got to VVR, what we'd eat when we got to a real restaurant in town, what we'd eat when we were done with this trip and had regular access to a refrigerator again, and what we'd eat if we went to a buffet. Etcetera. We talked a lot about food.

We made it to the second bear box late that afternoon. I held my breath as I walked towards it. I knew it was likely to be empty, but I also knew that without more food we were going to be in big trouble soon. I unhooked the latch on the front. I pulled the door open. Bare.

"Anything in there?" Margo asked from across the deserted campsite.

"Nothing," I replied dejectedly. "It's empty. There's even a note in here from the ranger asking people not to leave extra food behind. Bastard." I was disappointed. We would appreciate extra food, of any kind and in any amount. We weren't picky.

"It's OK," Margo tried to reassure me. "We've still got one more." This was the second of the three bear boxes we'd seen on Guthooks. We'd get to the third one tomorrow.

"Yeah," I replied. "One more." We sat down in the shade and drank some water. Both of us were hungry. This was going to be a long couple of days.

"Shall we go?" Margo asked.

"Yes, let's go." I stood up, and as soon as I did the whole world swam, with black threatening to engulf my vision completely.

"Are you OK?" Margo looked concerned, although I couldn't see that through the encroaching blackness.

"I just need a second," I said, trying to find my balance.

"I'm so hungry," I continued after about 30 seconds,

"every time I stand up I feel like I'm going to pass out. It's getting worse."

"How long has this been going on?" Margo asked.

"Since yesterday afternoon."

"Oh, sweetie. I hope we can make it to VVR."

The next day we got to the final bear box before VVR. We still had about two and a half days to go before we got our next resupply, and we were really low on food.

Margo walked up to the bear box. "Let me open it," she said. "I'm feeling lucky."

"OK," I replied. I crossed my fingers.

"There's something in here," Margo announced excitedly.

"What is it?" I asked, trying to get a look over her shoulder at our treasure.

"Macaroni, and some cheese powder stuff." She held up a one pound bag of dried macaroni, and a plastic baggie full of bright orange-yellow cheese powder.

"Excellent!" I can honestly say I've never been so happy about macaroni and cheese. "We can mix this macaroni in with our dehydrated dinners, and maybe we won't have to go to bed quite so hungry."

"This will make the difference," Margo said. "I think we're going to make it to VVR just fine."

The macaroni helped stretch our dinners. But we still had no snack food, and after lunch that day we'd be out of food to eat during the day. The only thing that we had left was a few ounces of dehydrated peanut butter. I'd bought this a few years ago after seeing an ad on the internet somewhere extolling its virtues. Then I tasted it, and it sat in my cupboard for the next two years. It's not that it was bad, but it definitely wasn't peanut butter, and it wasn't even really a good substitute. As we'd been packing up our apartment in preparation for this hike, I'd taken anything out of the cabinet that I thought we may eat and put it into one of the resupply boxes. We'd been carrying the dehydrated peanut butter for a couple hundred miles, because even out in the wilderness it wasn't really good enough to eat. But now, it looked like it would get eaten.

That night we put half the macaroni in our dinner and went to bed a little less hungry than we had the night before.

Mars and Coyote were on the same schedule that we were, and we wound up camping together most nights through the mountains. We met up with a young woman named Gazelle who was hiking the John Muir Trail between jobs, and she was moving at our pace as well. Our little group moved through the mountains at the rate of one pass per day. Everyone was looking forward to getting to VVR.

"So, you're moving up to Seattle?" I asked Gazelle. She'd told us earlier that she'd landed a new job, and was moving from our former home, the Bay Area, up to Seattle. "How does it compare with the Bay Area? Was it tough to find a job up there?"

"It seems like it's similar to the Bay Area in a lot of ways," she replied. "It's growing quickly, and housing prices are going up, but I still think it's a little cheaper than the Bay Area. Traffic seems like it's a little better too."

"Everyone who lives up there loves it," I said. "I haven't heard too many complaints about anything other than the weather."

"It was really easy to find work up there," she added.

"We're going to be in the market for somewhere new to live after this hike," Margo added. "We're just asking around and letting stuff marinate for now. But I wouldn't be opposed to Seattle."

"No, I wouldn't be opposed either," I said.

"Tomorrow night we'll be at VVR," Margo said, changing the subject. There were five of us sitting on the ground next to our tents, eating our dehydrated dinners. "I'm so hungry, I can't wait."

"Same here," said Gazelle, although she seemed to have a little more food left than the rest of us. "It's been a long haul. Six days since I resupplied."

"Tomorrow will be ten days for us," I said. We'd taken an unusual approach to the Sierras, trying to minimize the long hikes out to resupply. Our last resupply had been before Mt Whitney. Carrying enough food to be well fed for 10 days just isn't possible, so we knew we were going to be hungry by the end. Still, knowing you're going to be hungry is one thing. But actually being hungry, and still having to hike 15 miles a day over high passes, is something else entirely.

"Ten days," said Coyote, "that's pretty brutal. It'll be eight for us."

"I hope they have ice cream at VVR," Margo said. She'd developed a taste for milk shakes out here.

"And beer," I added. I needed calories, and beer seemed like a great way to get some. "I'm losing weight so fast up here. Check out my shorts." I pulled my waistband away from my waist, leaving a 3 inch gap.

"Yeah, I'm in the same boat," Mars chimed in. "I was losing weight in the desert, but since we've hit the Sierras, it seems to be falling off a lot faster."

"Tomorrow night we dine on the finest food a remote outpost in the mountains has to offer!" Gazelle nearly sang. It couldn't come soon enough.

Chapter 5: Cruising Thru the Sierra

Vermillion Valley Resort isn't actually on the PCT. It's on the other side of a huge lake. You can either hike to the northeast side of the lake, where a ferry will pick you up and take you over to VVR, or you can hike around the south edge of the lake. The hike around added a couple of miles, but it freed us from the boat's once per day schedule at this time of year. So we opted for the hike.

We got to VVR in the early afternoon. "I'm going to go pick up our box," I told Margo. I wanted to make sure our resupply box had made it there. If not, we'd have to figure out a different way to get food here. We were still starving, but we knew we would be eating soon.

"OK, I'll go see what there is to eat in the store." Margo headed off towards the little storefront. Our box had arrived, and after picking it up I sat on a bench on the front porch and looked through it to see what we had.

Margo came out a few minutes later, her arms laden with food. She had a couple Micheladas, that wonderful, salty Mexican concoction that combined tomato juice and beer. She also had a bag of Fritos and a couple ice cream sandwiches. We were starving, and flooding our systems with junk food felt phenomenal. We devoured everything as fast as we could, barely even taking time to breathe.

After finishing off our junk food lunch, we sat on the bench in a satisfied stupor.

"That was even better than I'd imagined," Margo said. She slumped on the bench sporting a lazy grin, her eyelids heavy.

"Yeah," I agreed, "but I couldn't eat as much as I wanted to. I think my stomach shrank."

"Well, there's plenty more in there. Plus we can have dinner at the restaurant tonight. I heard it's barbecue night."

"Mmmmm, barbeque," I moaned.

After a few more minutes, as our food coma waned, we decided to go set up our tent among all the other hiker tents in the sprawling dirt campground across from the store, next to the large parking lot. Fifteen minutes later we were both in the tent, napping away our first substantial meal in several days.

After a fun night at VVR that included a big communal campfire, we were planning on heading out the next afternoon to get back on the trail. The boat that we wanted to take across the lake left at 3pm, so we had a few hours to kill before it was time to go. We sat around in front of the store with other PCT hikers, talking about trail life, trail people, and the trail in general.

"Hey, long time no see!" I looked up and saw Nick and Jam coming towards us. Nick was still wearing the same outfit he had been wearing on day one, when I first saw him — purple shorts and a lime green shirt, colorfully contrasting with his bright red, unruly beard. They had come across the lake on the morning ferry.

"Hey!" I exclaimed, extending my arm for fist bump. "We haven't seen you guys in weeks! How's it been going?"

We caught each other up on what had been going on since we'd last spoken, in the desert before Tehachapi. The trail is strange like this. You get close to people as you hike with them on the same schedule for a while. Then someone takes an extra rest day, and you don't see them for weeks on end. Then, suddenly, they catch up to you and they're back into your world again. It's one of the things that is most fun about hiking this trail.

"What's your plan for the rest of the Sierras?" I asked, after we'd caught up on everything else.

"We're going to zero here tomorrow, and then head out the next day," Nick replied. "What about you guys?"

"We're leaving here in a couple of hours on the afternoon boat. I guess that'll put us a couple days ahead of you."

"I'm sure we'll see you again down the trail before too long," Jam said.

"I hope so," Margo said. "You guys were just about the first people we met on the trail, and we've missed you the last few hundred miles."

"Same here," Jam said. "But it's a long trail. We'll see you again." But we never did.

The boat ride back across Lake Edison was beautiful. Lake Edison is a huge lake, much bigger than most of the Sierra lakes. But as with other Sierra lakes, it's surrounded by stark granite peaks that seem to shoot up from the shore and climb thousands of feet straight up into the sky. As we rode across the lake, we admired the peaks, most with snow still adorning their flanks. We admired the gleaming lake, and the mix of trees and granite boulders on the shore that seem more perfect than even the most carefully tended Zen garden. We admired the wilderness that we were heading back out into, the wilderness where we would spend that night, and the next, and the next. This wilderness was really starting to feel like our home.

We were rested and well fed after our stay at VVR. We continued on our northward journey, feeling energized and better than we had in days. My pack felt light, even though it was heavy with the food we had picked up at VVR. We felt strong, nearly invincible. We were in great shape at this point since we'd been walking every day for over 2 months. We were well acclimated to the elevation since we slept at high elevations every night. Now that we had enough food in our systems, with plenty more calories on our backs, we glided through the rest of the High Sierra in pure bliss.

"I think this is the best view in the entire Sierra range," I told Margo. We were sitting on a granite slab, looking across Thousand Island Lake towards Mt Ritter. The lake didn't literally have 1,000 islands, but it probably had 30 or 40 little islands dotted across it's glittering, sapphire surface. Mt Ritter rose out of the crystalline blue on the other side of the lake, it's summit 3,000 feet up and still covered with late spring snow. Ground squirrels ran through the green meadows that surrounded the lake, sticking their heads up to look around, then racing across the meadow in search of whatever ground squirrels go off in search of. A large raptor sailed on the air currents high above our heads.

"It is stunning," Margo agreed. It was our second day out of VVR. "I could just sit here all day."

"Yeah, this is so relaxing," I agreed. "This stretch going through the mountains is so special. We're so deep in the wilderness, so far from everything, and surrounded by this beauty."

"It's a great feeling," Margo agreed, "to just be completely immersed in this stunning landscape. This lake is really pretty, but let's be honest, almost every view we've had over the last week and a half has been world class. We wake up in this beauty, we spend all day hiking through it, getting different vantage points, seeing each face of each mountain, moving through the landscape in slow motion. Then we go to sleep surrounded by the same beauty."

"Then we repeat the next day," I added. "And repeat and repeat. It's hard to believe how good a routine can feel, how relaxing it can be. How it just puts you in touch with a part of yourself that somehow gets lost in civilization."

"Yes, exactly," Margo agreed. "It's just an easy and peaceful life. Even though we're hiking 20 miles a day, it's the most relaxed I've ever been."

"We should have 3 more days left to get to Tuolumne Meadows, and then we won't be quite so high in the mountains. The mountains will start to flatten out, and the Sierras will be winding down. I hope it will still be pretty after that, but I think the best part of the trip will be behind us."

Tuolumne Meadows, in Yosemite National Park, was our next resupply stop. It was where the John Muir Trail (JMT) and the PCT separated from each other, with the JMT heading down into Yosemite Valley and the PCT heading northward towards Canada. It was also the end of the jaw-droppingly spectacular section of the PCT. After that, we'd move into terrain that was merely gorgeous.

"Well, we'll just have to enjoy it up here while we can," Margo said. "I wish we could camp here tonight. It's such a stunning spot."

"Yeah, it would be great to spend more time here. But Canada's calling, and we've got to keep moving." Soon, that wouldn't be the only thing that would keep us moving.

They came out of nowhere. At least that's the way it seemed. One day we were relaxing during a long, leisurely lunch, taking in the gorgeous scenery that surrounded us on all sides, with barely a care in the world. The next day, we couldn't stop for a drink of water without getting swarmed, with tiny buzzing wings assaulting our ears, tiny mouths biting into any exposed skin. It was mosquito season in the Sierra.

"What do you think about this spot?" I asked Margo. We were looking at a flat spot on a ridge several hundred feet above a lake that could be a potential campsite. "It's breezy up here, so at least the bugs won't be too bad." We'd barely been able to stop for a break that day, as each time we stopped we spent most of our time swatting at the tenacious mosquitos. We had even had to eat our lunch, which is normally a very relaxed affair, while we hiked.

"It's nice, but it's still pretty early," Margo replied. "And, there's no water close by."

"Yeah, five is a little early to be stopping." It was mid-June, so dark didn't set in until around 9pm. Our normal schedule was to hike until about seven or so. "The water is like a quarter mile back, which is a pain, but we'd only have to make the trip once to fill everything up."

"I say let's keep going down to the lake we'd planned on camping at," Margo suggested. "It might be a little buggier, but we'll deal with it."

"All right, let's go." We took off down the hill, towards the lake.

Some lakes in the High Sierra, especially the ones at higher elevations, are surrounded by granite slabs, often interspersed with granite boulders of various sizes. At these lakes, it's easy to find a good campsite in the flat spots nestled in among the granite. These lakes are nice. This, however, wasn't one of those lakes. This lake was at a lower elevation, below tree line, and a meadow surrounded it.

You may think that a meadow sounds pastoral and lovely, a perfect place to spend the night. Nope. Early in the season, as the snow is melting and there's water everywhere, "meadow" is really a euphemism for a marshy bog. If we pitched a tent in that marshy bog, it would be like trying to sleep in a partially filled bathtub with grass growing in it.

Even worse than that, though, are the mosquitoes. Mosquitoes love meadows. Especially wet, marshy meadows.

As we dropped towards the lake, this all became obvious to us. As Margo walked in front of me, I could see the black cloud of mosquitoes swarming around her head. I could tell by the loud buzzing that a similar cloud engulfed my head.

"This won't work for tonight." It was a statement so obvious that Margo just gave me an annoyed look. "At least it's still pretty early. Let's check where the next campsite with water is." I pulled out my phone and opened up Guthooks.

"All right, but hurry." Margo was swatting at mosquitoes in vain. The black cloud around her head would part to let her hand pass through, then immediately reform. "I'm getting eaten alive."

"Yeah, me too," I said, my right hand alternating between poking at my phone and swatting bugs away. "Uh oh. It looks like we can either camp at the river in half a mile, or go to the next water in 7 miles."

"It's 6pm, and I'm feeling a little worked. I'm not up for another 7 miles today," Margo said.

"Yeah, me neither. Let's go to the river and hope for the best."

We came up to the wide, flat river. We were still down in the same meadow we had been in at the lake. The flat basin allowed the river to spread out and flow very slowly. It was about 50 feet wide and looked to be waist deep. But with the weak, meandering current crossing it would be no problem.

Unfortunately, mosquitoes were still swarming us. It didn't look like we'd get a respite tonight if we camped at this river.

"I say let's cross the river and camp on the other side," I suggested. "At least that way our shorts and shoes can dry overnight. We'll just have to deal with the bugs tonight."

"OK, sounds good," Margo replied. "I see a nice flat spot with a fire ring over there."

We waded across the river. At this point crossing rivers was no big deal for us. We did it several times a day. If our shoes ever got close to drying, it wouldn't last long. We'd come to another river crossing, and they would get wet again.

"This spot looks good," Margo said when she reached the other side. It was a huge flat spot with a fire ring surrounded by some nice logs to sit on, right on the bank of the river. We were still getting swarmed by the bugs, but it looked like that was inevitable tonight. "You put up the tent, and I'll get a fire going. Hopefully the smoke will help with the mosquitoes."

"Then make it a really smoky fire," I suggested.

Twenty minutes later, we were sitting together on a log in front of our very smoky fire. You know how when you sit around a campfire, everyone moves around to avoid the smoky spot just downwind of the fire? Not tonight. Margo and I both sat in the thick white plume of smoke coming off the fire.

"Look, there's Phoenix and Fancy Pants," I said, looking across the river that we'd crossed earlier. "They've got some other people with them too." Six people were walking up to the river on the opposite bank, all of them wearing mosquito nets over their faces but still swatting at the air in vain.

They plunged into the river, barely breaking stride. When they got across to the bank where we were camped, they made a beeline for our fire.

"These mosquitoes are unbearable!" Phoenix wailed as she reached the fire. She stood right behind us in the plume of white smoke.

"It's a little better here in the smoke," I said.

"Then let me in there too," said Fancy Pants, walking up to our fire and crowding into the smoke plume. Soon there were eight of us all jammed together in that plume of smoke.

"Are you guys camping here tonight?" Margo asked Phoenix.

"I guess so. It's a long way to the next water, and this fire seems to help with the mosquitoes."

"Yeah, and who knows," I added, "the bugs may not be any better up ahead anyway. Once the mosquitoes come out, they're everywhere. We're just going to have to deal with them, I guess."

Phoenix, Fancy Pants and the rest of their crew got to work setting up their tents. We had a quick dinner that night, and everyone was in the shelter of their tents, under their mosquito nets, by 7:30. Mosquito season was upon us.

We had one final pass to get over before we made it to our next resupply. Donner pass is where the PCT enters Yosemite National Park. It's also the last time the trail goes up above 11,000 feet, and we expected it to be the last place we'd encounter snow. We sent our micro-spikes back home at our last stop, in Mammoth Lakes, so we'd have to navigate this pass with just our trail runners. But we weren't worried. Over the previous couple of weeks we had become experts at navigating through these mountains, snow or no snow. We were excited to cross our last major pass.

I slogged up the steep approach to the pass. Granite slabs lined the trail, interspersed with low grasses and tiny purple and yellow wildflowers. Sometimes the trail crossed over these granite slabs.

"They call this Sierra Sidewalk," I told Margo as we crossed a large granite slab.

"Sierra Sidewalk?" she looked momentarily puzzled, then smiled. "Yeah, I get that. It's way easier to walk on than anything else out here. No lumpy rocks or holes in the way, just a solid, flat surface. I like Sierra Sidewalk."

"Yeah, me too," I replied, smiling.

Up ahead, a lone figure trudged north, heading uphill towards the pass. We gained on him quickly as he wasn't moving very fast. A few hundred feet below the pass I caught up to him as he stopped to catch his breath.

"Good morning," I said. "How's the climb going for you?"

"Not bad," he replied. "Slow but steady."

He was an older guy — quite a bit older, actually — with an enormous white beard that reached nearly to his belt line. His eyes were bright, and the lines on his face made it obvious that smiling came easy to him.

"I'm Mike," I said, "and here comes my wife Margo behind us."

"Tinker," he said, sticking out his fist for a fist bump. "This is my second thru hike. I did the AT two years ago and loved it. I'm hoping I can finish this one."

"Of course you'll finish," I replied. "I hope we finish too." I pointed at my arthritic knee, still wrapped in a knee brace.

"I'm sure you will," he said. "I was 72 when I did the AT, and now I'm 74."

"74!?!" My jaw fell open. "That's impressive." We were over 900 miles into the trail. Whether or not he finished, walking 900 miles at 74 is a feat to be proud of. "I hope I can walk this far when I'm 74. How fast are you moving?"

"I try to do 16 miles a day," he replied. "I'm not sure if that's fast enough to get me to Canada."

Seventy-four years old, and out here hiking 16 miles a day? Through these rugged mountains? This guy was impressive.

"It might be close," I replied. "But even if you don't make it, you've accomplished something amazing out here. And anyway, you're almost through the best part of the trail."

"Really, you think so?" he said.

"The Sierras have been spectacular," I replied. "How could it get any better?"

"If there's one thing that I learned on the AT, it's how easy it can be to underestimate a long hike like this. You might be surprised by what's ahead."

"Yeah, I guess," I replied, though I was full of doubt. "Washington is supposed to be pretty. But Northern California and Oregon are all just long slogs through trees, with none of these stunning views that we've gotten used to. Plus, I think it dries out again in northern California, and we've got to worry about water, like in the desert."

"Well, I'm not sure I agree," Tinker responded. "I don't want to be too quick to judge what's ahead. And regardless, I really want to finish this hike. It'll be a travesty if I don't make it to Canada."

"You'll make it," I said, trying to be encouraging. "We'll see you up at the pass." And with that, I headed off towards the top of our last high pass.

I don't know what happened with Tinker. He was moving more slowly than we were, so we never saw him again after that. But, regardless of how he viewed the hike, being out there and giving it a shot at 74 had already made him an inspiration, and from my perspective his hike was already a huge success. I hope he made it to Canada.

We continued on over the pass and into Yosemite National Park. As we headed down from the pass, I felt a little morose. Yosemite was beautiful, but we would soon pass through it. The High Sierras, the part of the trail I'd been most anticipating, was ending. I thought about the beauty we had seen, and how unlikely it was

that anything left on the hike would compare.   I
wondered if the best part would soon be behind us.

Chapter 6: The End of the Sierra

We stood at the edge of the first road that the trail had crossed in over 300 miles. Since Kennedy Meadows, the trail had only passed through wilderness. It had gone up over steep passes, down into lush, pine covered valleys, past soaring peaks and pristine lakes. Crossing a road felt like the end of a long wilderness adventure.

"The post office is that way," I said, pointing up the road. "The general store is right next to it. Let's go get our resupply box, and maybe we can pick up something in the store too."

"I heard there's a grill there," Margo said. "I want pancakes."

We strolled down the road towards the post office/store/grill. An endless stream of visitors to Yosemite streamed by us on foot as we walked along the road side trail, and in cars that meandered slowly past on the road as their occupants soaked in the marvelous scenery. Everyone smelled so nice. Except, I assume, us.

"There it is," I said, pointing up ahead. "Look at all those hikers sitting at those picnic tables." There were about 15 PCT hikers sharing three picnic tables under the shade of some pine trees, just across the parking lot from the post office.

It wasn't difficult to tell the people crowded around the picnic tables were PCT hikers. At this point we had all been living in the wilderness for a couple of months, and that gave us a very distinctive look. Picture a stereotypical homeless person, and you're pretty close. We are all very dirty, and most of us have raggedy hair that, at this point, hadn't seen scissors in months. Our clothes are dirty, with permanent sweat stains criss-crossing our shirts that match our backpack straps.

Aside from being dirty, our clothing is distinctive in other ways as well. There are only a handful of shoes that 95% of PCT hikers wear, and only a slightly larger number of jackets. Backpacks are the same way. I'd guess 95% of PCT hikers carry the same 5 backpacks. And finally, almost every PCT hiker carries the same water bottle — a Smartwater bottle with a Sawyer inline filter screwed into the top. It was almost like we were all wearing a uniform. A very dirty, sweaty, stinky uniform.

That's all to say that, if you know what to look for, it's easy to identify a thru hiker. We had no trouble recognizing the members of our tribe, and they had no trouble recognizing us.

"Hey guys, can we squeeze in here," Margo asked, walking up to the least full of the three picnic tables.

Two men and a woman were going through their resupply boxes, repackaging things into Ziploc bags and getting their food organized so it would fit in their packs.

"Sure thing," one of them said, scooting over. Margo grabbed a couple spots for us while I went into the post office to get our resupply box.

Thirty minutes later, we had packed away the food for our next stretch and we'd eaten an order of pancakes and a couple of ice creams from the general store.

"Hey guys, what's up?" Ranch, who we hadn't seen since the desert, came over and sat down at our table. We exchanged greetings.

"Are you staying here tonight, Ranch?" I asked. We still had to figure out where we were going to sleep.

"Yep, I'm all set up at the campground over there. Tomorrow I'm going to hike down into Yosemite Valley. I got a permit to hike down there and climb Half Dome on the way!"

"Awesome," I replied. Half Dome is an epic hike. To get to the top of the gigantic granite dome, the last few hundred feet are over a steep, sheer granite face that's angled at about a 45 degree slope. There's no trail, no dirt, no trees, nothing but exposed slick granite. The National Park puts up a set of cables that you hang onto as you make your way up. It's the iconic Yosemite hike. "You're going to love it, and you're going to love Yosemite Valley."

"Are you guys staying here tonight?" Ranch asked.

"We are," I replied. "But tomorrow we're heading north towards Tahoe. We live in northern California, so we've seen Yosemite Valley plenty of times. You'll enjoy it for sure. But we've got to keep moving, because we've got a vacation coming up."

"A vacation from this?" Ranch asked, looking confused.

"Yeah," I replied. "We're going to a family reunion in Wyoming for a week this summer. I've got a brother and two sisters, and they all live out on the east coast so I don't get to see them very often. They've all got kids too. I've got nine nieces and nephews altogether, and most of them will be there."

"Wow, that's a big group of people. How are you going to get to Wyoming?"

"Our plan," I replied, "is to rent a car and drive out there. We've still got nearly a month before we'll go, so we're just going to see where we're at around that time. We'll have to figure out how to get to a big enough town to rent a car, but we'll be able to sort it out. We might wind up getting off the trail and heading to Redding or something."

"That sounds like a lot of fun," Ranch replied.

"Yeah, it'll be fun, and we're going to eat so much food!" Margo added. "I don't plan on doing much besides sitting on the couch and eating all week, with a little family time mixed in."

"Definitely no hiking," I added.

"That's going to cost you some time," Ranch observed.

"Yeah, it will. With the drive to and from Wyoming, we'll be off the trail for like 10 days. At least. That's why we've got to keep moving."

"Makes sense," Ranch said. "I'm heading back over to the campground. If you want to walk over there with me, I can show you where it's at."

"Sounds great," I replied. "Let's go."

The next day we continued our trek northward, heading towards Lake Tahoe. The stretch of trail between Yosemite and the town of South Lake Tahoe is still the Sierra, but it doesn't have the renown among the backpacking crowd that the stretch south of Yosemite has. Even though I'd lived in California for a couple of decades and had hiked in the Sierra quite a bit, I was unfamiliar with the stretch north of Yosemite. I'd heard it was nice, but in my mind it had always been second best to the section south of Yosemite that we had just hiked through. But I was learning that was a misconception; the section north of Yosemite was gorgeous.

"I can't believe how nice this has been," I said to Margo as we made camp high up on the side of a valley wall, with a view of Smedberg Lake far down in the valley below. It was the end of our second day out of Yosemite. "I was curious to see this part of the Sierras, but I had no idea it would be so gorgeous."

"Yeah," Margo agreed, "and it's so much less crowded than the John Muir Trail section we just went through. I'm loving it."

From our campsite, we could see Benson pass at the south end of the valley. We had crossed over that pass earlier this afternoon. To the north the valley continued, eventually dropping off towards lower elevations. There were peaks visible on all sides of us, but they differed from the enormous granite blocks that made up the peaks to the south. These peaks had looser, crumbly looking rock, striped with striations. The color was different too. Rather than the light gray granite we'd grown used to, they were much darker, with a reddish-brown tint to them. We could still see granite in places, but the geology was changing.

"These mountains remind of Colorado mountains," I said. "They definitely don't look like the mountains we've been hiking through for the past month."

"They're gorgeous," Margo said. "And the bugs aren't out up here on this ledge."

"I guess it's too windy for them here," I said. The mosquitoes had continued to plague us, and having a break from them for an evening was wonderful. We were still in the peak of the mosquito season, starting a smoky fire most nights to ward them off.

"I just wish it wasn't so cold," Margo said. The sun had just dropped behind the ridgeline, and with its disappearance the temperature had plummeted.

"We lose the sun too early in these canyons. And once the sun is gone... brrrr, bedtime." We were both wearing every piece of clothing we had, other than our rain gear.

"Hey, are you still putting sticks on your bear canister every night?" I asked, as Margo loaded her food into her bear canister, getting ready for the night.

"Every night," Margo replied. "And every morning, they're just where I left them. Not a single sign of a bear, or even a raccoon, bothering it." Disappointment was all over her face.

"I'm surprised we haven't seen one," I said. "Surely

142

we'll see at least one bear before this trip is over."

"I hope so," Margo said. "It would be so cool to see a bear. You know," she continued, "we only have 3 more weeks until our vacation. I can't wait. It'll be so much fun to see your family and to just sit on the couch and relax."

"And to eat," I added. "I'm going to eat more fruit than you can imagine."

"And salads," Margo agreed. "Anything fresh is at the top of my list."

"What's the first thing you're going to eat?" I asked. And from there, the conversation went down a very familiar path, for neither the first or last time on this hike.

"Look, there's Sonic and Fish up at that campsite," Margo said as we rounded a bend.

"Hey there!" Sonic yelled as she waved from the campsite she had found, up on a little plateau right above the trail. "Are you guys looking for a spot to camp? There's plenty of space up here."

"Yes, we are," I said. "We'll come up there and join you."

We jumped across a little stream and made our way to Sonic's plateau. It was a great campsite, a large flat area about 15 feet above a little stream, surrounded by large, thick trunked oaks. There was a large flat space with room for about 5 tents there, with a fire pit in the middle.

"Let's get a fire going," Margo suggested, as she

swatted at a bug on her arm. The mosquitoes were back with a vengeance and being camped so close to the stream only encouraged them.

"Great idea," Sonic agreed. "I'll help you out."

While I set up our tent, Margo and Sonic got the fire going. As usual, the smoke helped knock down the mosquitoes, and soon the four of us, plus Bandit and Raven who were also sharing our campsite, were sitting around it enjoying some relief from bug swatting, and some pleasant camp camaraderie.

"I'm excited to get to South Lake Tahoe tomorrow," I said. "I think we're going to zero there."

It had been almost a month since we'd had a full rest day. Before our long stretch in the Sierra where we'd run out of food, we had gone down into the town of Bishop and stayed with a friend of mine who, coincidentally, had moved there only a few weeks earlier. We took a zero at his place while we resupplied and caught up with him, but since then we had been walking every single day. Some days had been short days, or neros, but we hadn't had a completely hiking-free day in that long stretch. We decided we were due for one in South Lake Tahoe, so we had booked an AirBnB in town for two nights.

"Nice," Sonic said. "We're meeting my parents and my dog in North Lake Tahoe in a few days, so we'll take a zero when we get there. We'll spend one night in South Lake and then move on." Sonic's smile broadened at the mention of her dog. "But, tomorrow is actually my birthday."

"Lucky you!" Margo said. "You get to spend the night in a bed on your birthday!"

"And have a good dinner," Fish added. "We're having a little celebration at a brewpub in South Lake tomorrow night. You guys should join us."

"Absolutely," Margo said. "Just text us the details when you get cell service, and we'll be there."

"Same here," Bandit added in. Bandit was always up for a social engagement.

The sun was behind the canyon wall already, and the temperature was dropping. The fire warmed us a little, but even so, our sleeping bags were calling. "It's time to get into my sleeping bag," Sonic said.

"Yep, dusk is here. That's my bedtime too," I responded.

Ten minutes later the fire was out and everyone was in bed. It was 8:40pm.

"It looks like I overshot at the grocery store." I was in our AirBnB, standing in front of a giant platter that was overflowing with what must have been fifteen pounds of fruit. A watermelon, a pineapple, plums, peaches, grapes and apples were piled high. I thought that we had an insatiable craving for fruit, but it seemed like this was too much even for our bottomless stomachs.

"I don't know," Margo replied. "We've got a couple of days here. Surely we can at least put a dent in it."

"The fresh fruit is going to be great," I said. "But I'm so tired of the hiking food we have to buy at the grocery store." We had sent resupply boxes to about half of our town stops, but in the other half we had planned to buy our food in town. South Lake Tahoe was one place where we were buying in town.

"I know," Margo replied. "It's like there's only about 3 different things we can buy for dinner, and I'm tired of all of them."

"Ramen noodles, instant potatoes, and Knorr sides," I said, screwing my face up in disgust. "I'm sick of all of that too. I wish we would've sent a box of dehydrated food to every town."

"Me too," Margo replied. "How many more times do we have to buy food in town?"

"Too many," I said. "Hey, but at least we get to take a zero tomorrow. It's going to be so nice to wake up and NOT have to hike."

"I know," Margo replied. "And we've got a birthday party tonight. What a fun stop this is going to be."

"Speaking of," I said, "we should head over to that brewpub pretty soon. Do you want to take those bikes in the garage?"

When we walked into the brewpub, Bandit was already sitting at the bar. "Hey guys," he said. "Let's get a table. Sonic and Fish should be here soon. Oh, and I got Sonic a birthday card. Here, sign it."

We settled into a table, and Sonic and Fish showed up not too long after that.

We had a delicious, high calorie dinner. Everyone ate as much as they could put away. The beers went down easily and the conversation flowed smoothly.

"Once we get past Donner Pass in a couple of days, I hear the trail gets flatter," Bandit said.

"That's what I heard too," Margo said. "It will be sad to leave the high mountains, but a little less elevation gain every day sounds nice."

"I heard from someone who hiked the trail last year that northern California is the toughest part of the entire trail," Bandit said.

"Why is that?" I asked. "There's not as much up and down as there was in the High Sierra, right?"

"That's true," Bandit replied. "I think it's a psychological thing. You know, everyone was amped to get into the Sierra when we were hiking through the desert, and then every day in the Sierra was just epic. Now we're through all of that, but we're barely half done with California. It feels like a big slog ahead. I guess there's an emotional let down when you hit northern California."

"Ahh," I said, seeing where he was going. That let down had worried me too. "You've left the epic views behind, but you've still got to crank out the miles."

"Yeah, I mean we're not even half way through this hike yet. It's the first time a lot of people realize what they've got to do to finish before the snow starts, and for some that realization hits hard. You know, you do the math and realize you need to hike 19 miles a day or whatever, every single day, to get to Canada by mid-September. Whatever the number works out to be, it's daunting. Like I said, we're not even halfway, and it already feels like we've been doing this forever. Plus there are spots where we've got to worry about water again, and poison oak and rattlesnakes too."

"Great," Margo said. She wasn't happy about the rattlesnakes making a return appearance. I worried about the poison oak.

"I'll be sad to be hiking through forests all day, to

give up all those great mountain views we had through the Sierras," I added. "I think we're done going above tree line for a while, so I'm guessing there's going to be a lot of boring hiking through forests."

"Do you guys have a firm plan yet for what you're going to do after the hike?" Sonic asked, changing the subject. We had told her about our homelessness and how we were looking for somewhere new to settle after we finished the trail.

"Not really," I replied. We'd been throwing around ideas, but the end was still so far off that it seemed to exist in a different universe. "What about you guys?"

Sonic and Fish were in the same boat that we were in. They'd put all their stuff in storage, had quit their jobs, and were currently homeless. It wasn't an uncommon situation on the trail.

"I think we're going to try to land jobs in San Luis Obispo," Sonic said. "We were in Seattle before this hike. But we both went to Cal Poly, and we loved SLO. If we can get jobs there, we'd love to go back."

"It's a great town," I said, grinning. "It's on our short list too, but we're not sure about the job situation there. Is there work?"

"I think so," Sonic replied. "Cal Poly is a big employer, and there's a few software companies and engineering firms there. I'm hopeful we'll be able to find something."

I looked at Margo. "If we can find work, I'd love to live in SLO."

"I think I'd like it there too," she replied. "Maybe we should move it to the top of the list?"

"Maybe," I said.

We left about 10pm to ride our bikes home in the dark. It was the latest any of us had stayed up in at least a month.

Part 3: Northern California and Oregon

Michael Tyler

Chapter 7: NorCal Blues

"There's the freeway," Margo said as she crested a rise near Donner Pass. If you stopped and listened, you could hear the cars zooming by on Interstate 80 far below.

"We should be there in half an hour," I replied, "and then it's ice cream and junk food!"

Since we had left South Lake Tahoe a couple days earlier, we hadn't passed through any towns. But, where the trail passed under I-80 there was a highway rest stop. In that rest stop were a few vending machines, and we had heard one of them had ice cream, along with other typical vending machine food. It may not sound like much, but with our constant hunger we were always looking for extra calories somewhere. Getting those extra calories via ice cream is about as good as it gets. Even better, we would get to the rest stop right around lunchtime, which meant we could take our long mid-day break there.

As we walked down towards the freeway I

envisioned relaxing under a shady tree, eating high calorie treats in the warm afternoon. The anticipation was almost overwhelming.

The trail passes under the freeway through a big tunnel. As we got closer, the roar of the cars grew louder and louder, until we could barely hear each other talking as we neared the mouth of the tunnel. We walked under the freeway and came out into the sunshine on the other side.

"I can see the rest area right over there," Margo said as we emerged. A couple minutes later, we stood in front of four vending machines, loaded with delicious looking treats.

"Where to begin?" I wondered, surveying the spread. There was a coffee machine that didn't interest us too much, a soda machine, and a machine full of typical vending machine stuff like chips and cookies. And, as we'd heard, there was a machine with frozen treats like ice cream sandwiches and drumsticks. The bright lights of the vending machines were enticing, and in the throes of our hunger they were gorgeous. It was almost overwhelming. My mouth watered.

"I'm starting with ice cream," Margo replied without hesitation. I couldn't fault her. It was hot outside, we were hungry, and ice cream sounded wonderful.

After pondering her choices for a minute, Margo pulled out a dollar and fed it to the machine. The machine spit it back out, along with a cryptic looking error message on the little digital display. She tried again, with the same result.

"Here," I said, reaching for my wallet, "I've got a bunch of ones." I handed her another dollar, and again the machine rejected it. We went through every bill we had, and the machine wouldn't take any of them.

Margo face sank, her dejection obvious. "I've been looking forward to ice cream all morning."

"Me too," I replied. "But I guess it isn't happening today. At least we can get some chips and a soda. It'll be a better lunch than peanut butter and tortillas, right?"

"All right." Margo moved a few steps to the right and surveyed the junk food selection in the other machine. They had Fritos. You can never go wrong with Fritos.

But, when she tried to buy a bag of Fritos from the second vending machine, she got the same result. Again, we tried every bill we had in that machine, and again, nothing.

When we tried the soda machine, we weren't surprised when the same thing happened. After looking forward to some "free" calories all morning, it looked like our decadent lunch would not happen today.

"This is horrible," Margo said, as we walked out of the rest area building together, empty-handed. "I was so excited for some different food. It's all I've been thinking about all morning."

"Same here," I replied. "But there's nothing we can do. Look, there's a picnic table over there. At least we can sit at a table and have lunch. That's something right?"

We went over to sit at the rest area table. There was a woman with a backpack sitting at the table next to us with her shoes off and her feet up on the bench. She was obviously a PCT hiker.

"Hi, I'm Faceplant," she said as we walked up. "Did

you guys try the vending machines? I couldn't get any of them to work."

"We couldn't either," Margo replied. "I really want some of that ice cream."

"I guess we'll have to wait until Sierra City for that," Faceplant said.

Our lunch that day was peanut butter and tortillas, sitting on a concrete table next to a parking lot, with the buzz of the freeway loud in our ears. It was a horrible lunch. It had shattered our sense of anticipation.   The man-made, noisy environment made us feel anxious and on edge. The sun blasted down on the parking lot, with no shade in sight. We were used to enjoying our lunch relaxing among the trees, with the peaceful silence of the surrounding forest. Eating in a parking lot was much worse. And we didn't even get any ice cream out of the deal.

Northern California was off to a rough start.

"They lied," Margo said. "This isn't any flatter than the Sierras."

We were sitting at an empty campsite, leaning up against a downed log enjoying our lunch with Mars and Coyote. The dense forest provided plenty of shade. We were waiting out the mid-day heat, something we hadn't had to do in our month of walking through the High Sierras.

"It sure doesn't seem like it," I agreed.   "We're definitely lower though, you can tell by the heat." It was July now, and we were spending time at much lower elevations than we had in Sierras.

"In some ways this reminds me of the desert," Margo said. "It's not quite as dry, but there's definitely less water. It sucks to have to carry a few liters at a time again. And I think it's hotter here than it was really anywhere in the desert."

"It's a little demoralizing to know that the Sierras are behind us, too," I added. "We've left a great part of the trail, and now we have to spend a month hiking through the forests."

"It's a mentally tough section, that's for sure," Coyote said. "So far, it's the toughest section of the trail for me. I think I've got the NorCal blues."

"I'm feeling the NorCal blues too," I replied. "We've got a really long stretch now that, at least from what I've heard, doesn't have any of the marquee view points that we've been enjoying. When we passed Lake Tahoe we left behind those postcard views."

"So you're saying we've got to get all the way to Washington to get good views again?" Mars asked. "All of northern California and Oregon are boring forest?"

"I hope I'm wrong," I said, "but that's what I'm worried about."

"What are you guys complaining about?" Margo asked, jumping into the conversation. "The forest is great. It's our home now. I feel so relaxed and at ease walking through all that green. Don't you guys?"

"I guess," Mars replied. "But I'm not sure it can compare to those mountains."

"I don't think so either," I replied. "But I guess there's not much to do but make the best of it. For the next one thousand miles."

"Oh, by the way," Mars said, "I heard Yoda dropped out in Mammoth. Something about a stress fracture in his foot."

"Really?" I was stunned. We hadn't seen Yoda since the day before we climbed Mt Whitney, but we knew was a strong hiker, mentally tough and in great physical shape. I had been sure he'd make it to Canada.

"Yeah, he was devastated, from what I heard," Mars said. "It's happening to a lot of people. The crowd is thinning out. The NorCal blues are hitting some people harder than others."

"I guess so," Margo agreed. "I'm guessing we'll see another big drop off at the halfway point."

"Yeah, and we should get there around the end of next week, it looks like," Mars said.

"And right after that, we're taking a vacation!" I said. "We can't wait. We're going to eat so much food…"

"What time did they say we could check in?" I asked.

"Three o'clock," Margo replied. "And I can barely wait. I'm really looking forward to that shower."

We were in Sierra City, a tiny town in the low foothills of northern California. In the High Sierra, passes defined each day. That was the rhythm of the trail through those mountains; over a pass in the morning, and get set up for the next pass in the afternoon. Northern California had a different rhythm, playing out in multi-day patterns. We would spend days hiking up in the mountains, now lower in elevation, but still above the towns and roads in the valleys below. Then, every four or five days, we would drop down a couple thousand feet to a small town in a low-lying valley. Then there was always a big climb when we left town to get back up into the mountains, a few more days of hiking, and then a steep drop into the next town. Sierra City was one of the first of those towns we would hit.

"At least we can get lunch while we wait. I heard the general store down there has a grill. Do you want to go check it out?"

"Of course I want food," Margo replied. I'm not sure why I even asked.

The grill counter sat off to the side in the tiny, overpriced general store. The menu contained exactly what we'd come to expect at these kinds of places. Burgers, fries, chicken fingers – in short, nothing fresh, but plenty of deep fried calories. At the very bottom, the menu listed a thing called the hiker trash burger. One pound of hamburger, plus cheese and all the toppings. That sounded just about right.

"I'll have a hiker trash burger and an order of chili cheese fries," I told the guy behind the counter.

"That's a lot of food," he said.

"I'm pretty hungry," I replied. That was an understatement. "I'll take this liter of Dr. Pepper here too." Full sugar Dr. Pepper. What was the point of messing around with the diet stuff out here?

Ten minutes later, when they called my number, I saw that he was right about the quantity of food. It was a lot. Like a-feed-an-entire-village-lot. It turns out one pound of meat makes for a giant burger. The fries were enormous, a large basket that would have been enough for three or four people. They were covered in thick chili and chopped onions, and the whole thing was buried under a layer of melted yellow cheese. Eating all of this was going to be fun.

I was starving, so I dug in with reckless abandon. The burger was juicy and delicious, the fries a sloppy, wonderful mess. Everything tasted great, and I imagined that I could feel my body taking in all that food and using it to rebuild my tired, sore muscles. It felt great... at first.

Ten minutes later, and that sense of bliss had evaporated, replaced by something much closer to nausea. "Is there a bathroom in here?" I asked the lady at the general store counter. I had finished the giant burger. The huge pile of fries wasn't completely gone, but it was a lot smaller than it had been, with most of the cheese and chili sopped up and in my now swollen belly. I had eaten way too much food, and I felt terrible. I was sure puking was in my immediate future.

"Sorry," she replied. "There's one at the community center two blocks up the street."

There was no way I was walking two blocks in my current state. My stomach was so engorged I couldn't even stand up straight. I was afraid I was going to lose my cookies right there, all over the checkout counter of the general store.

I really didn't want to throw up. I mean, no one ever wants to throw up. But aside from the unpleasantness of vomiting, I didn't want to lose all those calories I'd just eaten. I figured I had something like three or four thousand calories sitting in my stomach, and I needed every one of them.

It took all I had to walk out the front door and around behind the building. I found a dirt parking lot with three or four cars parked in it, and a dumpster off to one side. That dumpster was my spot.

I walked over to the dumpster, still not able to stand up straight. I bent over and put my hands on my knees, hoping the waves of nausea would pass. I was in agony, my swollen stomach barely able to contain the enormous amount of food. But I really wanted to keep those calories. A few people passed by in the alley that ran next to the parking lot, looking at me suspiciously. I'm sure I was a frightening sight. A dirty, skinny, unshaven guy hanging out next to a dumpster, bent over, hands on knees, groaning. It was definitely not my finest hour.

I'd say it took twenty minutes to get to a point where I felt all right again, like I might be able to stand up straight. I didn't feel great, but at least I didn't puke. But I didn't know when I'd be able to eat again.

I went back into the general store and walked to our table in the back by the storage room. Margo was still sitting there, chatting with other hikers.

"Where have you been?" she asked. I told her about my ordeal.

"I don't know if I'll be able to eat anything for the rest of the day," I said. One of the major attractions of being in town is the opportunity to eat nonstop, so I wasn't happy about having my stomach out of commission for the rest of our stay here.

"Oh, you'll bounce back by dinner," she said.

I didn't. Although I really wanted to eat all the food I could while we were in town, I couldn't eat a bite for the rest of the day. I went to bed without eating, but I wasn't hungry at all.

"Are you guys thinking of going down there?" We'd just bumped into another hiker heading south on the trail. We were eyeing a lake about 200 feet below us, off the trail.

"We're going to give it a try," I said. "I think we're going to camp there tonight, as long as the lake isn't too nasty. What about you?"

"I'm thinking the same," she said. "Do you think the lake is going to be nasty?"

"Well," I said, "it's called Duck Soup Lake. That doesn't exactly bring to mind cool, pure, crystalline water, does it? And we've heard rumors that the water there lives up to its name."

"Duck Soup Lake?" She laughed. "I didn't know that. It sure sounds a little nasty."

"I guess we'll take a look and see," said Margo, and the three of us headed down the steep, loose slope towards the lake down below us off the trail.

"I'm Missy, by the way," Missy said as we headed down.

"I'm Mike, and that's Margo," I replied, gesturing towards Margo. "How far are you going?"

"Just from Chester to Sierra City," said Missy. "I missed this stretch when I did the whole trail last year, so I'm back to finish it, along with one other stretch up north that I'll do next. What about you guys?"

"We're doing the whole trail this summer," I replied, "or at least that's the plan."

"Awesome! How has the hike been so far?"

"It has been amazing. We've enjoyed every step." That might be a bit of overstatement, but not much. We really were having the time of our lives.

"What do you like best about it?" Missy asked.

"Just being outside every day is so energizing," I said. "I can't believe how good it feels to be surrounded by nature every day. Even on days when we don't have spectacular views, when we're just walking through the forest, being in nature constantly makes us feel happy and content."

"And it's such an easy, stress free feeling," Margo added. "It's really amazing how relaxed I am, all day, every day."

"I remember those feelings," Missy replied. "I know exactly what you're talking about, and I miss it so much. Enjoy it while you can. Once you're back to regular life, you're going to miss this."

"I'm sure that's true," Margo replied.

Well, here it is," Missy said as we came to the bottom of the steep slope and the shore of the little lake. "Duck Soup Lake. I can see where it gets its name."

The lake was small, a large pond rather than a lake. It was surrounded by pine trees, like most everything in northern California so far. No ducks were in the pond, but the "soup" part was definitely accurate. The water was murky, with small logs and leaves floating in it. A thin, almost invisible layer of some yellow dust, maybe pollen, covered the surface. The water was nothing like the water of the pure, crystalline lakes we had grown used to in the High Sierras.

"Are you OK drinking that tonight?" I asked Margo,

motioning towards the lake.

"What choice do we have?" she replied.

"The last water I passed is about 6 miles from here, if you're heading north," Missy said. "That's a long haul this late in the day."

"I don't have another 6 miles in me, so I guess it's duck soup for tonight."

"I'm feeling the same way," Missy said. "This isn't my first choice, but I'm not up for any more hiking this afternoon."

"I see a big tent site over there," Margo said, motioning towards the far side of the lake. "Want to join us there?" she asked Missy.

"Sure, sounds great," Missy said. We made our way over and set up our tents.

That night, the three of us gathered in the dirt between our tents for a dinner of dehydrated food reconstituted in Duck Soup.

"How's the trail from here to Belden?" we asked, curious as always about what lay ahead.

"It's typical northern California," Missy replied. "Lots of ups and downs, and then a huge drop down into Belden. This section was the hardest part for me last year. That's why I ended up skipping this section. There's something about northern California that's just mentally tough."

"We've heard other people saying the same thing," Margo said. "And we're feeling it too. I'm not sure what it is, but it's really been tough for us."

"I think it's because we've left the Sierras behind," I suggested, "and we know it's all downhill from here, figuratively speaking."

"I don't know about that," Missy replied. "I really enjoyed Oregon and Washington when I hiked them last summer. The scenery in Washington is really world class, and Oregon is fun because it's easy and fast. For me, the longer I lived this lifestyle, being free and sleeping outside, the more relaxed I got, and the more I enjoyed it. This hike isn't all about the scenery, you know. There are lots of other things to enjoy on a trip like this. You guys have some highlights and great times ahead of you, I guarantee."

"I hope so," I replied doubtfully. "I'm a huge fan of the scenery, that's the main attraction for me. If the Sierras are really the prettiest part, I'm just worried there's not much left to get from the trail over the next 1,400 miles."

"I'd be willing to bet you'll be singing a different tune by the time you hit Canada," Missy replied.

"How did you enjoy hiking the trail last year?" Margo asked.

"It was awesome," Missy replied. "I felt the same way you guys feel — like it was the time of my life. And after finishing, this winter at home, I only grew to appreciate it more. You guys know — it's an indescribable experience."

We finished our dinner, chatted a bit more about trail life and "regular" life, and at 8:15 we all crawled into our sleeping bags.

"Ahhhh, this is so comfy," Margo told me as she zipped up her sleeping bag to her chin. "I think it's the only time of day I'm completely comfortable."

"Yep, completely relaxed and completely comfortable," I agreed. "Sitting on the ground is all right, but there's always something poking at you somewhere, either on your butt or in your back. Walking is fine, but comfortable isn't the word to describe it. You're right – this is the only time when we're completely comfortable."

Margo didn't respond. I looked over at her. She was already sound asleep.

"I can't believe we made it here," Margo said as we walked up to the halfway marker.

"Halfway through the trail, and it's been almost exactly three months," I said. It was the first week of July, three months after our April 7th start at the Mexican border. "Hopefully we can do the second half a little faster than the first half."

"I think we can," Margo replied. "Just think how much weight we've lost so far. We're way faster now than we were at the beginning."

It was true. I'd lost about 40 pounds so far. My pack weighed around 20 pounds, plus or minus 3 or 4 pounds depending on how close I was to running out of food. That meant that right now I weighed less with my pack on than I had weighted at the start of the hike with no pack. Less weight definitely made it easier to move quickly, and we were covering close to twice as many miles per day as we had at the very start of the trail. The lower weight was helping out with my arthritic knee too, which hadn't really bothered me for hundreds of miles. I still wore a knee brace every day, mainly because I didn't want to jinx anything, but it seemed that all of the walking we were doing helped.

"Look, there's a register here," Margo said. She picked it up and paged through. "Look, Bandit passed by yesterday, he's just ahead of us. And here are Mars and Coyote, 2 days ahead of us."

"Anyone else we know?" I asked.

"A few people, but not many. I think most of our friends are behind us."

"Not only are we halfway," I said, "tomorrow we'll hit Chester, and we'll officially be on vacation!"

"I know!" Margo said, beaming. "I'm loving this hike, but a break is going to be so nice. Showers every day, a real bed, food..." Her voice drifted off she fantasized about things we've taken for granted our entire lives.

"It's 15 miles from here to Chester. If we can get in 10 more this afternoon, we'll have a nice easy hike into Chester tomorrow morning."

"Good," Margo said. "Once we get to town, I want to do a load of laundry and take a shower before we get on the bus to Redding."

Our plan was to take a bus from Chester, a tiny little trail town with little in the way of services, to Redding. Once we made it to Redding, we'd rent a car and drive to my family reunion in Wyoming.

"All right, we should have plenty of time," I said.

We took a few more pictures at the halfway monument. When I look back at those pictures now, they are the ones where we look the wildest. I hadn't shaved at all since the start of the hike, and my beard was unruly and wild. I'd trim it in Wyoming the following week, and it would never get back to that same bushy wildness it had at the halfway mark. Our clothes were filthy and worn out, and dirt made chaotic patterns across all of our exposed skin, including our faces. Our smiles were wide, our eyes bright. You may look at our pictures from that day and see a couple of dirty homeless people, but when I look at those pictures, I see two people who are extremely happy and very content.

The next day, we made our way into Chester by mid-morning. Though it was small, Chester was a little larger than the previous northern California towns we'd passed through, Belden and Sierra City. It was also a very friendly town. In an amazing display of generosity, the local church allowed PCT hikers to camp on their back lawn, and use their electricity to charge our endlessly hungry batteries and phones.

We set up our tent in the church yard, among about 10 other tents.

"That's it," I said, smiling. "Our vacation is on. We don't have to hike again for another week and a half." Margo and I high fived each other. We had made it through 3 months of living outside and hiking almost every day. We'd passed the halfway mark. And now, it was time for a break.

This is a story about hiking the PCT. Our vacation from our hike was wonderful, but I won't relay all the details here. As we had been planning, we spent lots of time socializing with my family, sitting on comfortable furniture, taking hot showers, and eating whatever fruits and vegetables we could get our hands on. Perhaps there was some ice cream mixed in there too, and maybe a trip or two to the candy store.

Beyond that, I had one conversation that I remember clearly and that is relevant to the story. My dad and I were sitting at the kitchen table alone. I have a big family, but I'm not sure where everyone else had gone at that point.

"It sounds like you guys are really enjoying your hike," my dad said.

"It's amazing," I replied. "We're so happy, and we're having the time of our lives."

"And you and Margo seem to be getting along great," he continued.

"Yeah, we really are. We always get along pretty well, but somehow we seem to get along even better when we're out there on the trail. I don't know if it's because we're always having to face obstacles together, or if it's the sense of peace that comes from living outside, or something else. But whatever it is, our relationship really couldn't be better."

"I'm so glad to hear that," my dad said. "Mom and I were really worried going into this. We really like Margo, and spending 24 hours a day, seven days a week together seemed like the kind of thing that might cause a serious riff."

Honestly, this had never occurred to me. As soon as my dad said it, I realized it was something obvious I should have been worried about. As I've told this story to a few people since the hike, they've let me know that they'd had a similar concern. But somehow it hadn't even occurred to me that spending 100% of our time with each other could cause problems.

What's even more surprising than the fact that Margo and I were getting along better than ever was that this wasn't unique to the two of us. After that conversation with my dad, I thought about other couples we knew on the trail. I hadn't known any of them before the hike, so I don't have a before and after comparison. But of the couples we knew, all of them, without exception, seemed blissfully happy on the trail.

A relationship counselor could probably shed some light on the psychology behind all the happy relationships on the trail. I'm sure there's some explanation; in fact, there's probably several different, complementary causes. Or maybe only happy couples would even consider attempting a thru hike together. But one thing is for sure: couples hiking the trail seem to be very happy couples. And, lucky for us, we were no exception.

Chapter 8: Fires

"It's looking pretty bad," Margo said, checking her phone as we drove west from Jackson, Wyoming. Our vacation was over, and we were on our way back to continue our thru hike. "The Oregon border is still closed, and lots of other hikers are complaining about the smoke in northern California."

While we were in Wyoming, several wildfires had broken out in northern California and southern Oregon. A few were close enough to the PCT that they were fouling the air on the trail, obstructing views and harming the hard working lungs of people hiking through it. One fire had resulted in a closure of the section of the trail where it crossed from California into Oregon.

"Well, it looks like we're going to have to skip a section to get around the fire closure for sure," I replied, keeping my eyes on the road. We'd just entered eastern Idaho, and the landscape was all agricultural. Green fields of low grasses that were tended to by giant rolling sprinkling systems whizzed by as we headed westward.

"I'm worried about the smoke too," Margo continued. "Do we really want to spend the next week breathing in smoke while we're walking up and down hills? We wouldn't even be able to appreciate the views with all the haze that's out there. Look at this picture." Margo stuck her phone in my sightline, showing me another hiker's Facebook post of an orange sun filtered through thick gray smoke. It did not look like healthy air.

"No, I don't think we do," I replied.

"It's a big section to skip over, but maybe we can come back and do it later in the fall. And as long as we have the rental car now, it's way easier to skip ahead now than it will be if we have to hitch hike around the closure."

"Yeah, or we can come back and get it next spring. Either way, it sounds like we're in agreement. Let's skip up to Ashland, just past the fire closure at the Oregon/California border. To be honest, I'll be happy to be done with northern California anyway."

We would skip a couple hundred miles of the trail to get around the smoke and the hassles of the trail closure. That decision meant we wouldn't have hiked a continuous path from Mexico to Canada, but we were OK with that. When we started the hike, being able to say that we completed the thru hike, with no qualifications or asterisks, was important to both of us. But as we hiked and got to understand trail life a little better, my perspective had changed. This hike was no longer some accomplishment, like scaling a peak, where the ultimate prize was being able to say I'd done it, and being able to check it off the list. Now, I was realizing that the things I enjoyed most about the trail, the things that made thru hiking special, had nothing to do with an "uninterrupted foot path", or even with completing the trail. People say stuff like "the journey is the destination" about a trip like this, and it always made my eyes roll. But I had to admit, I was starting to see where they were coming from. Living outside, stress free, with interesting people that you enjoy spending time with, were all things that were valuable about the trip, and were important to me. Being able to say "I walked all the way from Mexico to Canada" seemed like an arbitrary and pointless goal.

The next morning we dropped the car off in Ashland and took an Uber back out to the trail. The skies were thick with smoke in Ashland, but as we drove up into the mountains above town they cleared somewhat, and we began to see patches of blue sky above us. Our Uber driver dropped us off where the trail crossed the road, at an unremarkable bend. Just like that, we were back on the trail. We spent the rest of the morning figuring out how much of our fitness we'd lost over our vacation. Not much, it turned out.

That evening we found a nice campsite in a small grove of trees. We had the campsite all to ourselves. In fact, we'd been surprised at how few other hikers we had seen that day. "It feels fantastic to be back out here," Margo said between bites of rehydrated beans and veggies.

"Yeah, we did 20 miles today. That's great for our first day back from vacation," I replied. "And it seems like we're up above the smoke here, at least for now."

The sky had been clear blue all day. The worst of the fires burned to our south, so we were walking away from them. We didn't have much in the way of views, because we'd mainly been hiking through the forest, but even so the cleaner air was nice.

"It's been so flat so far," Margo added. "I mean, not like totally flat, but way less up and down than what we were dealing with in California."

"Everyone says Oregon is flat and fast. I heard some people are going to try to do the whole thing in two weeks."

"Two weeks?" Margo said, inquisitively. "That sounds pretty fast."

"Yeah, I guess it's like 30 miles a day, on average. That's a lot to do for 14 days in a row."

"We've got plenty of time, I say we take it a little easier and enjoy it," Margo suggested.

"That sounds like a great plan. Since we jumped up to Ashland, we're a little bit ahead of schedule so we don't have to push quite so hard. Still, as long as we've got some flat hiking, we should take advantage of it."

As we finished dinner and got ready for bed, Margo looked around the forest that surrounded us, up at the towering pine trees that reached above us towards the darkening sky.

"It feels great to be back home," she said.

I knew exactly what she meant. We were surrounded by trees, by the sounds of birds, by the smell of pine and rich soil, and it was all very comforting. It felt wonderful, and even better, it felt right. The forest felt like home.

"I don't recognize any of these people," Margo said. "I miss our old bubble."

We were sitting outside the store at Mazama village, part of Crater Lake National Park. It was our fourth night back on the trail after our Wyoming vacation. There were six or eight other PCT hikers sharing a couple of picnic tables, organizing resupply packages, eating high calorie treats from the store, and talking about trail life.

"Yeah, this is weird," I said. "It's like we're on a completely different trail. And everyone is moving so fast."

"I know," Margo replied. "I don't know if it's because everyone is trying to do Oregon really fast, or if we're just with faster people now, but we're not seeing the same people day after day like we used to. It seems like things are a lot more mixed up now."

I knew exactly what she meant. Oregon definitely seemed different. In the southern California desert, we never camped alone. Down there everyone wanted to camp by water, and so we all clustered together at water sources. It was very social, like a middle school sleepover night after night. In the Sierras, everyone wanted to camp at the bottom of the passes, so we could hit the high passes early in the morning when the icy snow was easier to walk across. So once again, we'd almost always share our camp at the base of the path with others. Even in northern California we seemed to be on the same schedule as a lot of people, and wound up seeing the same people night after night.

But Oregon was different. Now, suddenly, the social aspect of the trail seemed to be evaporating. Since we had been back from our vacation, we had camped alone every night. Not that I minded; I'm somewhat of an introvert, so all the socialization in California had worn on me, and I was happy for the break. But it seemed strange for the social nature of the trail to have changed so quickly.

We had also jumped ahead of lots of the friends we had made by skipping up to Ashland. We would meet new people all the time, of course, but there had been a loose group of 30 or 40 people that we had been on the same schedule with since the beginning of the trail. This loose group is known in trail lingo as a "bubble". Now we were in a totally new bubble. After 3 months of seeing the same general group of people, it was a bit of a shock. We were surrounded by people we didn't know.

"Well, regardless of how many miles we do tomorrow, we're going to have some great scenery. Tomorrow we walk around Crater Lake."

"I know," Margo replied. "I can't wait."

"Wow, what a view," I said, coming up to edge of the cliff that bordered Crater Lake. "The last time I hiked here I got snowed on, and I couldn't even see the lake through the clouds. This is stunning."

It definitely wasn't snowing today. The sky was a clear blue, with just a few fluffy clouds floating past. The air was warm and pleasant. Crater Lake stretched out before us, one of the most beautiful lakes I've ever seen.

Crater Lake is the deepest lake in the US. (Fun fact: on this hike, we would also walk by the second (Tahoe) and third (Chelan) deepest lakes in the US). The depth gives the water a stunning, deep blue color. The lake is actually a volcanic crater filled with water. The water level is a few hundred feet below the rim of the crater. The cliffs that rise up out of the lake on all sides are steep and rocky, composed of crumbly, dark volcanic rock. Their sharpness and dark color are in gorgeous contrast to the deep blue of the calm lake.

"I heard you couldn't even see the lake from the rim yesterday afternoon," Margo said. "It's hard to imagine, the lake is so big, and it seems like it's just right there." A new fire had started a few days ago in Crater Lake National Park, just a little ways north of where we stood. That fire wasn't nearly as big as the one to the south of us, but it was a lot closer.

"I hope the smoke doesn't get that bad today," I said. "Maybe we should go chat with that ranger and see what the deal is."

About a hundred yards away a park ranger stood next to a poster board with fire information.

"What's the word on the fire," I asked the smiling ranger as we walked up to her.

"It's burning a little to the north of the lake," the ranger said. "Are you guys hiking the PCT?"

"Yes," I replied. She knew immediately, because we had the look.

"You'll be west of the fire by a mile or two, but it'll probably be smoky as you get up there. Yesterday the smoke moved in over the lake in the afternoon.

Probably the same thing will happen today. So enjoy these views while you can."

"Any chance the trail will be closed by the fire?" Margo asked.

"No, not today," the ranger replied. "The fire is far enough from the trail that it's not a threat yet."

"Thanks for the info," I said, and we headed off to enjoy our walk around this stunning lake. We were happy that the fire would not have a huge impact on us. At least, not this particular fire.

Margo's birthday was a few days later, while we were still hiking through the southern part of Oregon. Fortunately, we were able to time our days in a way that allowed us to have a small birthday celebration. We were at Diamond Lake resort, although calling the place a "resort" is really quite generous. It consisted of a worn out hotel, a modest restaurant and a small convenience store. But at least Margo would be able to eat a birthday dinner that didn't require rehydrating, and she'd be able to spend the night in a bed.

That afternoon, after a shower and a load of laundry, we sat on the expansive patio adjoining the restaurant, enjoying the view of Diamond Lake. Rolling, tree-covered mountains surrounded the lake on all sides, and a few puffy, white clouds floated above us. There was a wall of smoke visible to the south across the lake, coming from the fire in Crater Lake that we'd walked past a couple of days before. But the wind was keeping the smoke to the south, and the sky above us was a deep blue.

Diamond Lake is quite a ways off the PCT, and it isn't known for being particularly welcoming to PCT hikers. There's no place to pitch a tent nearby, and the hotel rooms are on the expensive side, especially considering how much they were showing their age. We'd decided we'd make the effort to get here since it was Margo's birthday, but we were the only PCT hikers in sight.

"How was your dinner?" I asked Margo.

"Dinner was good," she replied, scraping up the last bits of pesto sauce with a piece of bread. "But it didn't fill me up. You can tell they're not used to having PCT hikers come through here. They're serving normal sized portions of food. I could've eaten two of those and still had room for dessert."

"Well, we should definitely get some dessert. Do you think they have cake?"

Ever since she was a little girl, Margo has one birthday tradition that she claims she's carried out every year. Her birthday cake is always chocolate, and she always squeezes fresh lemon juice on top of it. She's got a thing for chocolate, which I get, and lemon juice, which I don't.

"No, I'm sorry," the waitress said, after our chocolate cake request. "No chocolate cake. In fact, we don't have any cake at all. We've got ice cream. Do you want that?"

I glanced at Margo, and the disappointment on her face was clear. "No, thanks," she replied.

"Hang on," I said. "I have an idea." The little convenience store sat across a small yard. While Margo waited at our table on the patio, I headed to the store and bought a couple of Hostess Ding Dongs.

"Will this do the trick?" I asked, setting the Ding Dongs in front of her as I arrived back at the table.

"Perfect!" she said, smiling. She fished a slice of lemon out of the water she'd been drinking, opened up the Ding Dong, and squirted lemon juice all over it. As she took a bite and chewed, a smile crept over her face. She gazed out across the lake, at the families lounging on the grass between the patio and the lake front, at the dogs frantically chasing ducks near the shore. "This is the best birthday I could imagine."

We were flying through Oregon up until today. The terrain had been flat, and we had been putting in some of our biggest mileage days of the entire trail. But here, suddenly, the terrain had changed. The large volcanic cone of South Sister loomed in front of us to the north, with large patches of snow still clinging to its upper faces. Occasionally we could catch glimpses of Middle and North Sister, the other two volcanoes that make up the peaks of Oregon's Three Sisters wilderness.

Those peaks rose up on the horizon, still far ahead of us. Right now, surrounding us on all sides was reddish-brown lava rock. Sharp, crumbly, shoe destroying lava rock. We had been hiking through the jagged rocks for hours, and we were both exhausted.

"Are you doing all right?" I asked as Margo hobbled towards me. I was resting as comfortably as I could on a jagged piece of lava rock at the top of a mile-long climb.

Vast fields of sharp, unforgiving lava rock filled the views in every direction, broken only by the gigantic cone of South Sister to the north. There were no plants at all. There wasn't so much as a single blade of grass in sight.

"I'm worked," Margo said, dropping her pack and sitting down in the middle of the trail. "This has been our toughest day in Oregon so far."

"No argument there," I agreed. "Walking over this lava rock is a killer. The trail is hillier than it has been so far in Oregon too. This has definitely been a tough one."

"I know it's only 5pm, but I'm ready to call it a day. Do you think we can find a place to camp?"

I scanned the horizon. It wasn't looking good. We wouldn't be able to camp in the lava field. There was nowhere to pitch a tent. Motorcycle sized boulders of razor-edged lava rock were jumbled together in random patterns as far as the eye could see, with no flat spots at all in sight. And even if we had found a flat spot to pitch our tent, we wouldn't have been able to find any water. The starkness had a kind of beauty to it that I could appreciate. But it definitely lacked comfortable campsites.

"I think we have to keep going for a little bit more. Hopefully we'll get out of the lava soon, but unless we want to dry camp in the middle of the trail, I guess we just have to keep going for a while."

"OK, just give me five minutes," Margo requested. I could tell she was struggling. We were always tired at the end of the day, but it was rare for her to want to quit early.

We fought through the lava field for another hour,

rarely seeing anywhere comfortable to sit down, much less a spot where we could pitch our tent. Finally we came over a rise and saw a patch of trees a couple hundred yards ahead.

"Check it out," I said to Margo as she caught up with me on top of the ridge. "I think we can find a place to camp in there."

"Thank God." Margo looked as spent as I'd seen her in a couple of months, probably since the early days of the hike down in the desert when we were still getting our trail legs.

We walked into the patch of trees, and looked around for potential campsites. "Let's just camp here," Margo suggested, indicating a sloped, gravelly patch that was the first we'd come across. "I'm not sure I can go much further."

"I think we can do better than this," I replied. "This spot is pretty slanted, and rocky too. Let's keep looking."

Margo gave me a withering look and grumbled something I couldn't understand. I headed off in search of a flatter, more comfortable spot with Margo trailing a hundred feet behind.

"Can we just pick something already?" Margo was getting increasingly agitated. She was exhausted from what had turned out to be a grueling day. "It doesn't have to be perfect, you know."

"Let's just look over that next rise and see if we can do any better," I suggested.

"Whatever," Margo replied. In her exhaustion, her anger was clearly building.

We finally found a decent spot to camp, but by then

neither of us were in a good mood. Margo was exhausted, and her increasing annoyance with me had caused me to get agitated as well. As we got our camp organized, we squabbled about how we go about making decisions, and about how we generally live our life on the trail.

We ate dinner in silence that night and went to bed early.

"This may be the best spring we've seen on the whole trail," I said, dropping my pack next to a pristine pool filled from a large, gushing spring coming straight out of the lower flank of the mountain. South Sister loomed above us. The lava fields from yesterday had given way to meadows covered in short grasses accented by purple, yellow and white wildflowers. Lava fields still loomed above us on the flanks of South Sister, but they looked far less menacing in the distance.

"It's gorgeous," Margo replied. "I'm thirsty."

"Me too," I replied, dipping my bottle into the pool. "I'm not even going to filter this." I drank the cool, crisp water directly from my water bottle, without running it through my filter. The cool liquid slid down my parched throat, refreshing my dehydrated body in a way that only water straight out of a mountain spring can. Drinking that water was wonderful.

"Look, I'm sorry I got annoyed with you last night," Margo offered. "I was exhausted from crossing that lava field, and..."

"I know," I replied. "Yesterday was a tough day.

Don't worry about it."

We sat in silence for a minute or so. The refreshing spring water combined with the gorgeous view encouraged us to relax and enjoy the moment.

"You know," I said, "what's most surprising about that tiff last night is how rarely it's happened on this trip."

"It's true," she said. "It seems like we get along better out here than we do at home."

"I agree," I said. I told her about the conversation my dad and I had when we were in Wyoming, about how he was worried spending so much time together would endanger our relationship.

"Wow," she said. "I guess I never really thought about it like that, but I can see where he's coming from."

"Yeah, me too. But think about all the couples we've met on this hike. Do any of them seem to be having relationship problems? It's true that you never know what goes on when people are alone, but I get the impression that everyone gets along really well."

"Yeah, I know what you mean," Margo replied. "It seems universal. It seems counterintuitive, but there must be something about doing this that brings people closer together."

"Counterintuitive from the perspective of spending 24/7 together, I guess," I said. "But, maybe if you think about it from the perspective of facing daily challenges and overcoming lots of adversity together, it makes sense."

"I guess so," Margo said. "I mean, the proof is in our couple friends out here. And in us."

"Who would've guessed that the PCT is relationship

therapy," I said jokingly.

"This trail is amazing."

In fact, we were only beginning to understand the ways this trail would change us over the course of the summer, and beyond.

"There it is," I said, as we crested a rise and got a stunning view of Mt Hood. The mountain's flanks, covered in patchy, late summer snow rose up over the ornate, multi-gabled Timberline lodge.

"I see the lodge," Margo replied. "Somehow it looks familiar."

"I just read it was used as the hotel in 'The Shining'. That's probably why it looks sort of creepy."

"Yeah, but we're going to eat so good!"

We had first heard about the buffet at the Timberline lodge in a little town in southern California called Agua Dulce. We were having breakfast with Numbers, a volunteer at the amazing Hiker Heaven. Numbers had hiked the entire trail the previous year and was giving us the scoop on what to expect.

"One thing you definitely don't want to miss is the buffet at the Timberline lodge on Mt Hood. That buffet is epic. People will be talking about it 500 miles ahead of time." That was in late April, so we'd had this meal on our radar for almost 3 months. Now it was just a few minutes away. We were, as always, famished.

"When is your dad meeting us?" Margo asked.

"I got a text this morning saying he'd be at the lodge around noon, which is perfect. We should get there just about the same time."

"Thanks so much for making the drive out here, Dad," I said between bites of dessert. I had four different confections on a plate in front of me, and I was savoring every bite. "It's great to see you, and I think we're going to have a great hike tomorrow."

"Yeah, it's great to see you," Margo pitched in. She hadn't even started on dessert yet, she still had a luscious looking couscous salad studded with brightly colored tomatoes and peppers in front of her. "We sometimes feel a little disconnected out here."

"It's great to see you guys too," Dad replied. "I'm excited to be part of this adventure you guys are on. I heard from Ken this morning. He and David will be here at 7am tomorrow morning. They're excited about the hike too."

My uncle Ken and my cousin David both lived in Portland, a little over an hour drive from the base of Mt Hood. The five of us planned to hike the stretch of the PCT from the Timberline Lodge to Ramona falls, a popular day hike. Dad had made the drive out from Utah to join us.

"It should be a really pretty hike," Margo said. "I just hope you guys can keep up."

"Peanut butter and tortillas? Is that a common lunch for you guys?" my uncle Ken asked. We sat on a ridge above a huge gully at the base of Mt. Hood, enjoying our lunch. A large, fast-flowing river with white water caps cut down the bottom of the gully a few hundred feet below us. The mountain loomed above us, rising 4,000 feet above our lunch spot.

"We have peanut butter on tortillas every single day," I replied. "A guy we camped with one night in the first couple weeks of the hike gave us one — he had too much food and was trying to unload some weight. We gave it a try, and from there we were sold. It's part of our everyday routine now. They're high calorie, they don't spoil, and they're delicious. And we're able to find them in every grocery store, no matter how small or poorly stocked. It's the perfect lunch."

"Interesting," Ken replied. I could tell by his expression that I'd lost him somewhere, probably at the "delicious" part.

"How are you guys liking this hike so far?" I asked my cousin David.

"It's beautiful up here," he replied. "I really should come out here more often. The wildflowers are stunning, and the contrast with the rugged slopes of the mountain is dazzling."

"I'd say it's the prettiest day in Oregon so far for us," I replied. "Lots of Oregon up to here is pretty flat, and you're mostly just walking through a forest. I really enjoy the mountain views. Although I have to say, I'm starting to enjoy hiking through the forests too. There's something very soothing, very comforting in them. If you would have asked me a month ago, I would have told you forests are about the most boring places on the planet. But I guess I'm getting used to being in them."

187

"I realize it sounds sort of weird," Margo added, "but the forest really feels like our home now. We lie in bed at night and look up at the trees above us. The birds wake us up in the morning with the sunrise. It's all so soothing. It touches a part of your soul that you almost forget you had when you spend most of your time in man-made environments."

"It sounds like you guys are really enjoying this adventure," Ken said.

"It's the experience of a lifetime," I replied. That wasn't an understatement.

From there the conversation moved to politics and world events. This was the summer of 2018, a time when the nation was divided political issues, and those divisions seemed somehow deeper and more fundamental than they had in the past. The five of us all shared the same general political leanings, which leads to comforting, but uninteresting, conversations. What was unusual about this particular conversation was how out of touch Margo and I were with politics and the news in general.

"Where on the political spectrum do most PCT hikers fall?" David asked.

"Believe it or not, I don't know," I replied. "I mean, I assume they tend to be environmentalists. That would make sense. But I'm really not sure."

"What do you mean 'assume'," Dad asked. "You guys have nothing to do but sit around and talk, right? You must talk politics sometimes."

"Well, we have to walk too, Dad," I replied, stating the obvious. "But I get what you mean. We spend lots of time sitting around, shooting the breeze, but somehow politics doesn't really come up."

"That's surprising," Ken said. "With such a variety of people from around the world, there would be interesting conversations."

"Maybe it's just the groups we hang out in, but I can't think of a single political conversation we've had on this entire trail," I said.

"I think part of it is that people just aren't paying attention to that stuff," Margo said. "Yeah," I added, "I think that's a big part of it. We've got this healthy lifestyle that leaves you with this relaxed and happy outlook, completely free from stress. If we pay close attention to the news, or even spend time scrolling on Facebook, it makes us sad. Seriously, it's an effect you can feel immediately. It's so immediate and obvious, and so unpleasant, that everyone just sort of instinctively avoids it." "We've also got other things to think about," Margo added. "We worry about where we're going to sleep that night. We worry about running out of food, dying of thirst, being attacked by bears. The evil doings of some authoritarian idiot across the country don't' really crack the top ten of our worry list."

"Wow," Ken replied. "This hike is sounding better and better all the time."

"It was so great to see you," I said as Dad loaded his tent into the trunk of the car. "Thanks for making the drive out here. "

"It was great to see you guys too," he said. "It's fun

to be at least a part time participant in this hike you're doing."

After our hike together yesterday, Dad had camped with us at a spot where the trail crossed a small dirt road just north of Ramona falls. It was the third hike we'd done with him that summer, two on the PCT and one during our vacation in Wyoming. We didn't know it then, but we'd get one more chance to hike with him before the summer was over.

"Tell Linda thanks so much for mailing us our resupply boxes," Margo added as she gave Dad a goodbye hug. "You guys have no idea how much help you've both given to us on this hike. Taking care of the truck and helping with our resupplies makes our life so much easier. And being able to connect with family during this experience — it does more for our psyche than you'll ever know. Thanks so much."

"My pleasure," Dad replied. "I'm sure it does as much for me as it does for you."

I'm sure it didn't.

Part 4: Washington

Michael Tyler

Chapter 9: Bridges and More Fires

"We made it!" I high fived Margo as she came off the Bridge of the Gods, the trafficky bridge where the PCT crosses the Columbia river, leading us from Oregon into Washington.

"Two states down, one to go," Margo said excitedly as she returned my high five. "Washington is supposed to be really pretty, so hopefully we have a lot to look forward to."

"Hopefully we can enjoy it," I replied. "There's a couple of fire closures, and who knows if more are on the way."

It was a terrible year for fires on the PCT. The situation had only grown worse in northern California, as a new fire had started in the northern part of the state the previous week, and had grown into what was at the time the largest wildfire in state history (an even bigger fire later that fall surpassed that record yet again). A couple fires still burned in Oregon. In Washington, there were currently two closures on the PCT ahead of us that we would have to hike around, eventually. But we still had a couple hundred miles before we had to worry about them.

"There's really nothing we can do but walk north," Margo said, "and hope for the best."

"And keep our eyes on the news," I added. The PCTA website was great at keeping us updated on the fire situation all along the trail. We never felt like we were in any danger of being caught in a fire, we were mainly worried about the impacts of the far-reaching, lung-clogging smoke.

We headed north through the dense Washington forest. Raspberry and salmonberry bushes lined the trail, with thick growths of ferns and moss interspersed. Overhead, a mix of conifer and deciduous trees reached toward the blue, cloudless sky overhead. It was a lush forest, exactly what we had been expecting from Washington. We walked in silence for a couple of miles enjoying the change of scenery on the Washington side of the Columbia River.

A couple that looked to be in their early 60s came toward us, heading south on the trail. "Are you guys thru hikers?" the guy asked.

"We are," I replied. "We started at the Mexican border on April 7."

"That's great," he replied. "How's the trip going so far?"

"The trip has been amazing," Margo said through a broad grin. "It's been so much more than we'd expected."

"We're really excited for Washington," I added. "We hear it's one of the best stretches of the trail."

"Where are you from?" the guy asked.

"We were living in the San Francisco Bay Area before this hike," I replied, "but we gave up our place and put all our stuff in storage for this hike. I don't think we're going to go back there."

"We lived in the Bay Area for a while," the woman replied. "We raised our kids down there. But we moved up here when we retired, and we've never looked back."

"I can see why you like it up here. It's really beautiful," I responded.

"We love it here. We've got a great lifestyle. It's so much more relaxed than the Bay Area, just a much easier place to live. And it is beautiful, as you can see. If you guys are looking for a place to land after the hike, I'd seriously consider Washington."

"Hmmmm," I said, glancing towards Margo. "Maybe we should." It was about time to get serious about figuring out what we were going to do after the hike.

A couple miles further along the trail, I heard a loud cracking sound just off the trail, down a steep hill. I looked towards the sound, and a small bear was ripping the bark off a downed tree, looking for bugs. He was about 50 yards away, and completely unaware I was there.

I walked back along the trail as quietly as I could, looking for Margo. I walked toward her with my finger on my lips in a "Shhh...." gesture. "There's a bear just up ahead," I said in a stage whisper when I got close to her.

"No way!" her eyes grew wide with excitement. Together we walked the hundred yards back to the bear as quietly as we could.

"There it is," I said in a whisper, pointing towards the bear. It was still messing around with that same log. Then it looked at us.

It was a smallish bear. Not so small that we had to worry about its mother being nearby, but definitely not full grown. Its fur was a dark brown, almost black. Its round ears sat on top of its fuzzy head, giving the distinct impression that we were looking at a large teddy bear. It stared at us, and we stared at it, all of us frozen for about 10 seconds. Then it galloped off into the woods noisily.

"Wow," Margo said after the bear was out of sight. "That was amazing! I can't believe it took this long to see a bear."

"After all that bear canister booby trapping you did in the Sierras," I said, "now we finally see one all the way up here in Washington. I can't believe it took this long to see one either. Finally!"

"What an awesome day," Margo said, beaming.

The next night we camped in a stand of trees right next to a little creek. The weather was perfect, clear blue skies and a warm evening. The mosquitoes were mostly done for the year. We were enjoying our rehydrated dinner, luxuriating in the peaceful ambiance of the forest.

"Today was a tough one for me," Margo said, putting down her bowl as she finished her dinner. "I'm not sure why. I guess there's more up and down here than there was in Oregon, but even considering that I'm feeling pretty tired."

"Same here," I replied. "I can't figure out why either. We hiked 22 miles, which we ought to be used to by now. I think what's tough for me is just doing those kinds of miles, day after day. It's not the physical challenge so much, it's just mentally tough."

"I know! It's like we work all day to get to camp... 10 miles more to camp.... only 5 miles to camp... 2 miles, we're almost there!" Margo ran through the litany of emotions we both experienced every day, "and then the next day, we start over from scratch. 20 miles to camp."

"Exactly!" I agreed vigorously. "It's mentally exhausting. It didn't bother me before, and we've been doing the same kind of miles since northern California. I wonder why we're both feeling it now?"

"It's probably because we know we're in the final stretch. We can see the light at the end of the tunnel, and we're focusing on that."

"You know," I said, "when we're done with this, we're going to look back at it fondly. There will be a time, probably soon, when we're back in normal society and we will wish we were still out on the trail."

"For sure," Margo agreed. "We really need to just enjoy the moment out here. Because once it's gone, once this hike is done, it's gone for good."

"It's tough though. The daily grind, and the

thoughts of the comforts of home… it's hard to ignore those thoughts."

"Speaking of home," Margo said, deftly changing the subject, "how are you liking Washington so far? What do you think of that couple's recommendation to move up here?"

"I love it," I said. "The wilderness is gorgeous. Maybe we should seriously consider Washington after the hike. People love living here, and I think there are tons of jobs, especially in Seattle. You wouldn't have any trouble finding work there."

"I agree," Margo said. "And it's about time to start figuring out our post-hike life, I guess. We'll be done in less than a month."

"OK, I say we put Seattle at the top of the list."

As we talked, dusk settled in. The air took on a chill that had been mostly absent for the past couple of months. We'd started to notice the days getting shorter. In the Sierra the sun didn't set until almost 9pm, and often we'd be in bed in full daylight, before the sun hit the horizon. Now it was just past 8pm, and darkness was rolling in quickly. The days would only get shorter as summer continued to wane. We got into bed. I lay in my soft down sleeping bag looking at the trees towering above us, their tops barely swaying in the gentle breeze. The sounds of the forest — birds singing, the shuffling of leaves as a squirrel searched for dinner, a branch snapping underneath a deer hoof — eased us into another night of deep, contented sleep on the PCT.

"Look at this. Blueberries on both sides of the trail as far as we can see!" Margo was thrilled. It was berry season in Washington. We'd seen berry patches here and there hiking through Oregon, but nothing could compare with the way they lined the trail in Washington. Sometimes we'd see raspberries, the occasional salmonberry, but blueberry bushes were definitely the dominant plant here. All day long we'd pick them off the bushes lining the trail as we walked.

"Do you want to take a break here and eat some?" I asked.

"Yes!" Margo flung her pack to the ground. She took about 3 steps off the trail and sat down right in the middle of a large patch of blueberries. "I'm going to demolish this blueberry patch." A look of pure joy spread across her face.

I followed Margo's lead and dropped my pack on the trail, finding a seat in the middle of another patch a few yards away. Ripe blueberries covered the bushes. These blueberries were smaller than the ones in the supermarket, but they packed a lot of flavor into those little packages. They tasted nothing like grocery store blueberries. No, these were wild, free-range blueberries, and we could tell the difference with every bite.

We sat in the bushes on the side of the trail for a solid 15 minutes without speaking at all, eating blueberries as quickly as we could pick them. Finally satisfied, I looked around. The surrounding bushes were still full of berries. If we had sat there for another half hour eating berries, we wouldn't have been able to eat them all.

Margo smiled at me from her spot in the bushes a

few yards away, teeth purple with berry stains. "I can't imagine being any happier than I am right now," she said.

"This is amazing," I said as Margo walked up to the ridgeline. I was sitting on a boulder, munching on a handful of almonds. "Look at that basin!"

"Wow," Margo said, dropping her pack and sitting down next to me. "It's so green down there."

We were in the Goat Rocks wilderness in central Washington, one of the highlights of the state according to everything we had heard. If this initial view was any indication, everything we had heard was right. It was gorgeous. The ridge we sat on ringed a large, deep basin. A lush green carpet of low grass covered the lower part of the basin, punctuated by broad colorful patches of wildflowers. The rim of the basin was a sharp ring of peaks that sailed skywards into high, rocky summits in several places. From where we stood, we could see three separate waterfalls flowing down from the high peaks into the basin. A few patches of snow still studded the upper slopes of the peaks. It was one of the most picturesque places we'd seen anywhere along the trail.

The only thing that spoiled the effect was the haze in the air. It didn't completely obscure our visibility here, but there was definitely a smoky quality to the air. Both our eyes and our noses told us that the fire wasn't too far away.

"We're heading right towards the fire," I said. "The

smoke will probably get worse when we go over that ridge." I motioned towards the other side of the basin where we could just see the brown stripe of the trail hitting the ridgeline about half a mile away.

"When do we hit that fire detour?" Margo asked. The fire was, in fact, right on the PCT up ahead, so about 10 miles of the PCT was closed. We'd have to take an alternate trail to get around the fire. Word was it was a tough detour on a poorly maintained trail, and we would have to spend the better part of a day hopping over downed trees and fighting through brush.

"I think it's another 8 miles or so ahead. From what I've heard, the scenery only gets prettier as we go through Goat Rocks, so hopefully we'll have some good views. But I'm worried about the smoke."

"Well, let's enjoy what we can see while we can see it," Margo suggested, wisely. "There's really nothing more we can do."

We hiked around the big bowl, the trail clinging to the sides about halfway between the lush green bottom and the towering peaks dotted with large snow fields. After an hour or so, we were climbing up towards the ridge on the other side of the bowl.

"Wow, it's smoky over here," Margo said, gazing out across the newly visible landscape. The smoke was much thicker, giving us maybe a quarter mile view. The filtered sun had a deep orange-red tint in the haze.

There was a large camp on the ridge, several big canvas tents with lots of tools and equipment around. A crew was camped up there, doing some pretty heavy trail maintenance work. A guy from the camp approached us.

"It sure is smoky," I said as he drew closer, stating the obvious.

"Yeah, you should've seen it yesterday. Crystal clear in the morning, then the smoke rolled in early in the afternoon. I guess it just depends on the wind direction."

"I can tell it's gorgeous up here," I said, even though I could only get a hint at the beauty through the smoky haze.

"Normally from this ridge you can see Mt Adams right there," he motioned to the south, "and Mt Rainier right there. It's a stunning view on a clear day."

"I can only imagine," Margo said, her disappointment obvious.

"What do you know about the fire up ahead?" I asked.

"The trail's closed in another couple of miles. The official detour is pretty tough, a lot of downed trees, and up and down through a lot of mud. But if you just head down to Packwood Lake, you can hitch directly into Packwood from there. I'd recommend that, if you're wanting to go to Packwood anyway."

"That sounds great," I said. "We're planning on staying in Packwood tomorrow night, so we'll give that a shot." I was all for avoiding what was sounding more and more like a brutal detour.

We continued on through the smoke, across a section appropriately known as the Knife Edge. The trail wound down along a rocky, exposed ridge with steep, severe drops on either side. We could see the beginnings of the basins below through the smoky haze, and the outlines of snow peaks with late summer snow left on their flanks. We could see just enough to know that we were in a really special place.

"I'm definitely going to come back here some day," I told Margo as we surveyed the landscape. "I can tell this is an amazing place, even through the smoke. I want to come back and see it when the air is clear."

We took the easier alternate trail down to Packwood Lake. We got a ride down into the tiny town of Packwood with a backpacker on his way home from a couple of solo days in the wilderness. That night, we slept in a comfortable bed in a quaint hotel in town. But I would have rather slept up in those gorgeous mountains we had walked through earlier that morning.

"They run how far?" Margo asked, looking incredulous.

"One hundred miles," the guy said. He was standing next to the trail with a giant, very expensive looking camera. The sky was overcast, and a very slight drizzle kept everything just a little damp. The forest was lush, with a groundcover of ferns and berry bushes between the soaring trees. "It's the Cascade Crest Ultra-marathon. I'm one of the official photographers."

"And they pass right by here?" I asked.

"Yeah, this is about mile 25 right here. They started at 9 this morning, so the fastest people should start coming by soon."

"Great," I said to Margo after we bid the photographer farewell and were walking along the trail. "Our peaceful day in the wilderness is going to be interrupted by a bunch of trail runners."

"It'll be fine," Margo said. "Actually, it might help to break up the monotony of hiking a bit."

Within fifteen minutes the first of the runners passed us. "On your left!" we heard as the lead runner came up behind us. We stepped by to let him pass and continued on our way.

"That guy was flying considering he's already 25 miles into a 100 mile run," Margo said after he'd passed. I guess that's why he was in first place.

For the next hour or so, solo or pairs of trail runners would pass us every 5 or 10 minutes. They were all business, clearly trying to not only to finish this ridiculous race, but trying to do it quickly.

We stopped for lunch at an empty campsite right next to the trail. As we enjoyed our tortillas and peanut butter, we waved as trail runners passed by. The frequency and size of their groups were increasing as time went by. The runners also seemed to be getting more amiable as it got later in the day.

Just before we were about to pack up and start hiking again, a group of four, two men and two women, came running down the trail. We waved and smiled, and one of the guys stopped to chat with us.

"Are you all really running 100 miles today?" I asked.

"Well, we won't finish today," he said. "The cutoff time to finish is tomorrow afternoon at 5pm. Even the fastest won't finish today. The winner will probably finish around four or five am tomorrow morning."

"Do they set up tents or something where you can sleep?" I asked.

"No," the guy said, chuckling at my ignorance. "There's no sleeping. We run until we finish."

"You're going to run overnight?" This sounded horrible to me. "I think there's rain in the forecast tonight. Not this light drizzle, but, you know, real rain. Cold rain."

"Welcome to Washington," he replied, smiling. "Are you guys hiking the PCT?"

"The whole thing," Margo replied. "We started on April 7." It was currently the last week of August.

"I don't know how you guys do it," he replied, sounding genuinely impressed. "That's an amazing accomplishment."

"What are you talking about?" I said, incredulous. "Running 100 miles through the mountains without sleep is way tougher than what we're doing. You guys are really hard-core. We're just out for a walk."

We'd repeat a similar conversation several times over the next few hours. The runners were all overflowing with positive energy, despite the dreary, drizzly weather. I'm sure if we'd seen them at mile 95 it would have been a different story, but at mile 25 or 30 their legs were fresh and their energy levels were soaring. They added a happy energy to our day.

We came up to a ridge where the trail intersected a small dirt road. An aid station was set up there, with volunteers handing out carb-heavy snacks, water and plastic cups full of local craft beer. As we hiked up towards the ridge, the volunteers cheered for us.

"We're not part of the race," I said, stating the obvious. We had our giant backpacks and the general homeless-esque look of thru hikers. The runners, who had all showered within the past 24 hours, were carrying nothing more than a couple water bottles and maybe a packet of Gu. We couldn't have looked more different.

"That's OK," the volunteer guy who looked like he might be in charge said. "You guys deserve this as much as they do."

I didn't really agree, but I also wasn't about to argue. "Thanks so much!" I beamed as I took a plastic cup of bracingly hoppy IPA from the guy. The trail provides, as they say.

"Yeah, this is wonderful," Margo agreed, taking a bite off a giant hunk of watermelon. "You guys are great, and the runners have been so friendly. There's so much positive energy out here today."

"It's a great break from the routine for us," I added, as I finished off the IPA. "I was worried that sharing the trail with all these runners would disrupt our hiking groove, but I was wrong. It's been a ton of fun. This has been a great day for us."

"We've really enjoyed talking to the runners as they've passed," Margo said, "and it's really energized and inspired us."

"From what I've heard, the feeling goes both ways," the volunteer said. "What you PCT hikers are doing is inspiring as well."

Since we'd been in southern California, I'd always felt weird about getting praise for hiking the PCT. I mean, what about it is inspiring? We had dropped out of society and become homeless, just so we could pursue a selfish passion. It was self indulgent, plain and simple. We weren't curing cancer, or saving babies, or being productive in any way. It didn't seem like an accomplishment to me, but more like an indulgence. But I had a hard time articulating that. And I'm not sure anyone really wanted to hear it anyway. I guess people just enjoy being inspired, and who was I to rain on their parade?

As Margo and I settled into our tent after dinner that night, we heard the first drops of real rain hit the rain fly. "I hope all those runners are OK tonight," she worried.

"It's going to be miserable," I said. "It's going to be cold and wet and dark, and they're going to be over 50 or 60 miles into their runs. I can't imagine how tough that will be."

"It was a great day, though," Margo said. "That was probably the most fun I've had while we were hiking since the Sierras."

The pitter-patter of raindrops on the tent lulled us to sleep. We were cozy and dry in the tent, but we would get a taste of the runners misery soon enough.

"It sure sounds like it's raining hard," Margo said as she wiped the sleep from her eyes the next morning.

"It always sounds worse in the tent than it really is, but even so… I don't think it's going to be a very fun day."

I stuck my head out into the morning. It was more than drizzle, but at least it wasn't a full on downpour. I pulled my head back in and got dressed inside the tent. It was a real challenge with two of us in there, since the tent is just the right size for two people if both are lying down peacefully, flat on their backs. Anything more active than that and the tent quickly became unbearably close quarters.

"Let's just pack up as quick as we can and start walking," I suggested. "Hopefully the rain will let up, and we can stop for breakfast somewhere down the trail."

"OK," Margo agreed. "How far do we have to go today?"

"Snoqualmie Pass is 24 miles away."

"And there's a hotel there, right?" Margo asked hopefully.

"Yep. In fact, I think if we can get there today, we should just take a zero tomorrow. We're like halfway through Washington. I think we'll have about two weeks left after Snoqualamie, so that would probably be our last zero."

"Sounds great!" Margo said. "Twenty-four miles today, and a zero tomorrow. Hopefully it won't rain on us all the way to town."

"I'm starving," I said. It was after noon, and the rain was falling even harder than it had been that morning. We never got a break in the weather to stop for breakfast, and it didn't look like we'd be able to find a dry spot for lunch, either. We were both running on just a handful of almonds, thrown down our throats as we walked through the rain earlier that morning.

"Me too," Margo said. "I say we just stop under the

biggest tree we can find and have lunch."

"All right," I said. "It won't be dry, but maybe we can find a spot that's not quite as wet."

"How about that one back there," Margo said, indicating a tree back off the trail about 20 yards. We trudged through the damp undergrowth and muddy forest floor to the tree. We were a little protected from the rain underneath it, but drops continued to fall from the leaves down onto the hood of my rain jacket. I was hungry enough at that point that I probably would have sat down in the middle of a lake if it meant I could eat lunch.

"Let's just eat as quickly as we can and get moving," Margo said. "I'm cold, and this rain jacket isn't holding up. The rain is starting to seep through."

"Yeah, my hands are freezing," I said. "I can barely move them, much less do anything with them. I hope I can eat my tortilla."

"This is pretty miserable," Margo said as drops falling from the branches above her splatted onto the hood of her jacket. "I don't know how much more I have in me."

"We just have to get to Snoqualamie," I said. "At least we'll have a room there, we can dry things out and warm up."

"Yeah, but what about the next storm that hits?" she asked.

"You've got a good point," I said. "It's almost the end of August. Once September hits, risk of rain goes up, and by mid-September it's even worse. Plus it's going to get colder. We could start to see snow. But, we've got less than 300 miles left to go. I think we should just hurry; the quicker we can get to Canada, the less likely we're going to have to deal with bad weather."

"And the sooner we get to start sleeping in a regular bed, eating regular food, and being normal people," Margo added.

"I know. All that stuff sounds wonderful…"

"Especially on a day like today," Margo interjected.

"Yeah," I continued, "especially on a day like today. But, just remember, as painful as this feels right now, we're going to miss it when it's over."

"I know, I know," Margo agreed. "I'll miss this when I have to commute to work every day. When I'm sitting in an office, rather than hiking through a forest all day. It's easy to recognize that, but with it raining and miserable like it is today, it's hard not to be excited about being done."

"Even on a regular day," I added. "I've been noticing that as we're getting close, I'm getting more and more excited about finishing. I know I'm going to regret wishing this time away when it's over, but it's just irresistible. We're so close, the end is right there on the horizon, and it's almost impossible not to get excited about it."

"I know," Margo agreed. "But for right now, I'm just ready to get to that hotel room. Are you ready to go?"

Chapter 10: Walking to Canada

The first day of September dawned gray and cool. Pear Lake reflected the gray skies, giving the entire basin an imminent sense of fall approaching.

"It's chilly this morning," Margo said as she pulled herself out of the tent, already layered up in every piece of clothing she had with her.

"Yeah, chilly and gray," I agreed. "I hope there's no more rain coming our way."

The weather had been clear (or at least rain-free) since we left Snoqualmie Pass 5 days earlier, but the sky was constantly threatening another wet day. We'd heard September was when the weather would change in northern Washington, and our goal was to hit the Canadian border before it turned too sour. Time was running out.

"Are you feeling any better this morning?" I asked.

"A little," Margo replied. "My stomach is still a little upset, but I think I'll be all right to press onwards." A bout of nausea had hit Margo yesterday afternoon around the time we'd made it to camp. She had gone to bed even earlier than normal last night.

"Great, I hope it holds up," I said. "Just be cautious, though. We're only a day past Steven's Pass, but it's four days from here to Stehekin. If we keep going, we'll be pretty remote if you start feeling sicker and have to get a doctor or something."

"Yeah, I know," Margo replied. "I think I'm OK to keep going to Stehekin, but let me have some breakfast and see how I'm feeling."

An hour later, we were on our way north towards Stehekin when I heard Margo call out from behind me. I waited for her to catch up.

"I don't know," she said. "Walking doesn't feel good. I'm feeling really sick."

"Do you want to keep heading to Stehekin?" I asked. From the look on her face, I knew the answer before I even asked the question.

"I think I need to go to a pharmacy," she said, dejectedly.

"There's nothing back at Steven's pass except that tiny convenience store. But if we get back there, we'll be able to hitch down to Leavenworth. Do you want to give that a shot?"

"I don't want to," Margo replied. "But I think I have to. How far is it back to Steven's pass?" she asked.

"I think we can get there tonight if we really push it. If you need to take it easy, we can take it slow and get there by tomorrow morning easily."

"OK, let's go," she said. "We'll see if we can make it there today, and if not I'll be OK until tomorrow morning."

"The big drawback is that it's going to slow us down by a couple of days, and it's September," I said. "The weather is coming."

"I know," she replied. "But what can we do?"

"Well, since we're backtracking anyway, we could go from Leavenworth over to Chelan, and then take a boat directly to Stehekin. That would keep us on our schedule, and it would also get us around that fire closure right before Stehekin."

Stehekin is a little resort right on Lake Chelan, the third deepest lake in the US (after Crater Lake and Lake Tahoe). A fire that closed the PCT the 10 miles before Stehekin meant that everybody had to take a detour and a boat to Stehekin. We would just be taking a different detour around the fire, and a longer boat ride.

"How much of the trail would we miss if we did that?" Margo asked.

"About 50 miles worth," I said. "Fifty miles of pretty scenery, from what I hear."

The decision was tough. We'd already skipped around the Oregon-California border because of the fire closure, and skipping more of the trail, especially in such beautiful country, didn't sit well with either of us. But we also didn't want to be out on the trail in late September. In the end, we decided the boat ride was the best bet.

The two hour long boat ride was full of stunning views. Lake Chelan is a long, narrow lake, so although the trip up the lake was long, we could see both shores of the skinny lake the whole way. Peaks lined the shores, rising up out of the lake and into the blue, cloudless sky above.

Most people on the boat were out for a day trip up to Stehiekin, where they'd spend a couple of hours before taking the same boat back to Chelan in the late afternoon. As always, when we were around a bunch of 'normal' people, we worried that we were offending everyone with our aroma. I'm sure we were, but no one appeared to notice. Either that, or we were so used to being shunned that we no longer noticed it.

Just before lunchtime, the boat pulled into the dock at Stehekin. Stehekin is a tiny place, but the setting is surreal. The town is nestled below the jagged peaks that surround Lake Chelan, right on the shore of the lake. The entire area is completely cut off from the outside world by road. The only way to get to town is by boat or float plane. The road that leaves town runs about 10 miles, up to where it hits the PCT, but it doesn't connect to any other roads. We'd take a bus up that road back to the trail when it was time to leave.

The town consisted of a restaurant, a small general store, a post office and a national park service office. We would sleep at a national park campground just up the hill that night, but our first stop was the post office.

"This is our last resupply," I said, as we ripped open the box on a picnic table on the lake front. Large birds in V formations glided through the air just above the lake in search of fish.

"It's hard to believe," Margo replied. "The trip is coming to an end."

"It is hard to believe," I agreed. "Remember in the desert, we felt like this whole experience was endless. Like we were going to wake up and walk through the wilderness everyday forever. And now, it's almost over."

"It's sad," Margo said. "But at the same time I'm excited to go back to normal society, and all that it has to offer. Fresh fruit, real coffee, daily showers..." "Yeah, that's all going to be nice. But there's so much about this hike that I'm going to miss."

"Like what?" Margo asked.

"I'm going to miss the freedom we have out here. Even though sometimes it seems like banging out these big miles is a job, in reality it's a really free life. We live on our own schedule, stopping when we want, spending hours reading or napping in the middle of the day if we want. It just feels like the kind of freedom that isn't even an option in regular society."

"And the lack of stress," Margo added. "We've got nothing to worry about, other than making it to Canada. I don't think I've ever felt so relaxed in my life."

"Being able to eat whatever we want, whenever we want is pretty fabulous too. There's really no other time in your adult life when you can eat an entire bag of Oreos in one sitting and know that it's actually doing your body some good, rather than killing you slowly."

"The people are great too," Margo continued. "Even though it seems like it's a lot less social here in Washington than it was down in the desert, all the hikers we talk to seem like they're happy and healthy, and really enjoying themselves."

"Just like us.　Happy, healthy, and enjoying ourselves."　It couldn't have been more true.

I ripped open our last resupply box and organized it into two piles, one for each of us.　"You know what I'm going to miss the most, though?" I asked.　"Sleeping in the forest, surrounded by the trees and birds.　Waking up and going to sleep with the sun.　That's the part that makes me feel the most at ease, like some deep, evolutionary part of my brain understands that's how we're meant to live our lives."

"I couldn't agree more," Margo replied.　"I'm most definitely going to miss living in the forest."

"You guys get skinnier every time I see you," Dad said as he gave both Margo and I a hug.　We were a mile from the Hart's Pass parking lot, the last major road in the US.　Dad had very generously brought my truck to Washington so Margo and I would have a way to get home after we finished our hike.

"It won't last much longer," I replied.　"The weight's going to start coming back as soon as this trip is over.　Which is only a couple of days away."

"And hopefully that unruly beard is going to come off, too.　How do you feel about the hike coming to an end?" Dad asked.

"It's weird," I said.　"It's getting cold and walking day after day is really getting monotonous.　We both know we're going to miss this experience once it's over, but at the same time we're both sort of eager to get it done."

"Everyone doing this hike is in the same boat," Margo said. "Down in southern California, everyone camped together at the water sources. People were still getting their trail legs, so most people weren't doing huge miles and long days yet. We spent a lot more time socializing."

"Up here," I continued, "people are mostly in a hurry to get done, it seems. Everyone can feel the pull of the Canadian border, and everyone knows the bad weather is coming. People are walking from the first light of day until the sunsets, eating dinner in the dark a lot of the time. It's just a lot less social than it was down south. It seems like everyone just wants to finish."

"Yeah, and we're in pretty much the same boat," Margo said. "You can feel fall in the air. It's getting chilly. We've had a couple days of rain. It just seems like, with the seasons changing, it's time to wrap this up and get on with our lives."

"We're really trying to live in the moment," I added. "We've enjoyed this so much that going back to society, and back to work, will really be tough. But going back to a warm, soft bed and a daily shower is going to be so nice. It's a weird mix of emotions."

"You guys will really appreciate the shower," Dad replied. "You stink."

We started walking the mile back towards the parking lot. I've been outdoorsy most of my life. I have my dad to thank for that. When we were growing up in the mountains of Colorado, he made it a point to take my brother and I out on hiking and backpacking trips regularly, instilling a love and respect for the outdoors in us at a young age. That love and respect has not only endured into adulthood, it has grown. I often think of those trips we took as kids when I'm out in the wilderness.

This summer I was able to spend more time with my parents, and especially with my dad, while he hiked three separate stretches of the trail with us. Being able to experience even a small part of this adventure with him, spending good quality time with him outside, was a high point in a summer that was full of bucket list worthy highlights.

I thought about all of this as we walked towards the trailhead together. I tried to form those ideas into words, but fell short. "It's so great to have you here for this," I said to Dad as we walked. "I think I've seen you more this summer than any summer since I left home."

"It's my pleasure," Dad replied. "Doing this trip vicariously through you guys has been a delight."

"It wasn't completely vicarious," I replied. "You hiked the first mile with us, that big section around Mt Hood, and now this. Almost the last mile. And we really appreciated you and Mom's help with mailing our resupplies. I don't think we could've done this trip without you."

"Like I said, it's been my pleasure. Be sure and savor the last couple of days to the border."

"We'll try," I replied. The Canadian border was calling.

We came around a corner, and there it was. The

border.   The monument.   The thing we had been walking towards all summer.   One minute we were walking through the forest, just like we'd done for countless hours before, and the next, we were there.   The official end of the PCT.   The day was overcast and cool, with just a light drizzle keeping everything damp.   The air was cold enough that we had on all of our clothes, including our rain gear.

"We made it!" Margo's smile was broad, and I could tell she was ecstatic.

"Yes we did!" We high fived and dropped our packs next to the monument.

Monument 78 is similar in structure to the monument in Campo that we'd touched back in April to launch this experience.   It's five pillars of varying heights.   The lowest is maybe a foot high, and the highest is about 7 feet high.   The pillars at this end are made of a reddish-brown wood that fits in well with the heavily forested setting.   Dense trees surround the monument on all sides, except for a clear cut strip about 10 feet wide stretching off into the distance on both sides that marks the US-Canadian border.

There are no roads at the border at all.   We'd have to hike another 8 miles into Canada to get to the first road, so our day wasn't over.   But our official PCT hike was at its end.

We spent several minutes taking photos to commemorate the end of the trip.   These photos are a great contrast to the ones we took at the beginning of the trip, at the monument in southern California.   We'd both lost a lot of weight, and it showed in the photos.   My beard was thick and full, although it never got back to the crazy mess that it was just before our break around the halfway mark. My hair, which I'd shaved off at the beginning of the trail, was unruly.   The biggest similarity in the pictures is my knee brace. I had started out with it at the Mexican border, and I'd worn it all the way to Canada. My knee felt great, and I was pretty sure I didn't need the brace at all. Walking all those miles, day after day, had done a lot to reverse what the doctors had told me was a one way decline.

Five months on the trail had given us an inner glow that's hard to describe, but is instantly recognizable in those pictures we took at the monument. It's a look many PCT hikers have. I think it stems from the peace and freedom that, for most people, comes from a summer of living in the wilderness. When I look at those pictures from the monument, I see two incredibly happy people, completely at peace.

"Cheers," I said, cracking open one of the two beers that we'd carried here to toast our achievement.

"Cheers," Margo replied, popping the top on her beer. It was 11 am.

"Let's have lunch," I suggested. "It'll be our last peanut butter and tortilla lunch on the trail."

"And our first one with beer," Margo replied. She was beaming. We were both ecstatic.

"I can't believe we made it," I said. "My knee held up, the weather cooperated, no animals attacked us. All that stuff we worried about before and during the hike didn't even come close to stopping us. We made it to Canada."

"I can't believe how great this summer has been," Margo added. "I'm so glad we did this. I never would have thought that I'd find living in the woods, not taking showers, being cold, and hiking day after day so fulfilling."

"I couldn't agree more," I said. "It has been epic. Remember when we started down in the desert, those early days of the hike?"

"Of course," Margo replied. "Remember how warm and sunny it was."

"Yeah, and remember how everything looked," I said, looking around. "This really couldn't be more different. There we saw desert scrub, sand, and everything was brown. Here it's so green, just calling it green feels inadequate. We've got pine trees and ferns instead of desert scrub. And a wet, muddy ground instead of dry sand. It's a long way from the beginning to the end. It's hard to believe we walked from that dry, desert place to this lush, wet place."

"And think about everything we passed through in between," Margo added. "We've seen so much this summer, been through so much. It's almost more than I can process right now."

"And it's not just the scenery that's changed," I continued. "Think how much we've changed too. Even just physically, look at how much weight we've lost. And our legs are ridiculously strong."

"When I started, I worried about how often I'd be able to take showers," Margo said, "and about the cold, and wild animals. None of that stuff is even in the top ten list of concerns I have now. There's no doubt, we've changed."

"I can't believe how much I came to love the forest," I said. "By the time we hit Oregon, it felt like home, like a place I belonged. I wonder how long it will be before we lose this feeling. Do you think there's any way we can keep this feeling after we're back in civilization?"

"I hope so," Margo replied, "because I'm very happy. I'd love to hold on to it."

Epilogue

This is such an improvement," I said. We were sitting on the deck of the house we'd rented a week earlier, finishing dinner, looking out at the redwoods. "I think we're going to be happy here."

"I think so too," Margo replied.

It was about a month after we'd finished our PCT hike. After all the discussion on the trail of where to live after the hike, we'd decided to stay in northern California. Margo had found a job she liked in that area. But, rather than commute into San Francisco every day, she'd found a job near Santa Rosa, an hour or so north of the city. We'd found a house out in the middle of the forest, on the shores of the Russian River.

"Are you sad that our PCT hike is over?" I asked.

"I miss it," Margo replied. "It's been more than a month since we finished, and you know how it goes. The pain and suffering fades in your memory, and all that's left is memories of the good times."

"I'm so happy we could hike it together," I said.

"This is definitely an experience that we'll remember for the rest of our lives. And to be able to do it with you, and know that we have it to reflect on forever in the future…well, there's really nothing more I could ask for."

"I feel the same way, and I'm sure it will only get better in our memories as time passes," she added. "It's great we got along so well out there, too. You know, any little problem really could've spiraled out of control into a full blown conflict, but that never even came close to happening."

"It's amazing that out of all the couples we knew out there, everyone seemed to have a similar experience, relationship-wise. I guess that's just the way the trail works."

"Yeah, I guess it is," I said. "What was your favorite part of the trail?"

"I liked it all, in different ways. But the desert was really great."

"Why the desert?" I asked. As people prepare for the PCT, most dread the desert, and look at it as something to get through before the "real" mountains begin.

"It was so fun," Margo replied. "It was beautiful, not at all what I expected 'desert' to look like. But really it was the people we met there that made it special. Most everyone was new at this, and we were all getting to know each other. Every night was like a middle school sleepover."

"Yeah, I know what you mean," I replied. "It was a really fun section. And, at that point, the whole summer was spread out before us. It seemed endless. It seemed like we would just wake up every morning and walk through the wilderness for the rest of our lives. I really liked the desert too."

"But what was your favorite section?" Margo asked.

"I have to say the Sierras," I replied. "Even though I'd hiked that part before, it's just a special place. And going through with all the snow made it both exciting and beautiful. Being able to share it with you was my favorite part.

"I feel like Washington got the short end of the stick, though. It was gorgeous, but we were so focused on finishing the trip that we didn't enjoy it like we probably should have."

"Plus," Margo added, "there were all those fire closures up there. Maybe we should go back and check out some of those places again next summer."

"Yes!" I nearly shouted. That sounded like a great plan. "Count me in."

We finished our dinner, but sat there on the patio looking at the sun set behind the redwoods, sipping a luscious Sonoma county cabernet.

"Do you think that was the best summer of your life?" I asked, realizing it was a loaded question.

Margo paused for 15 seconds. "I think I'd say so," she replied thoughtfully. "I can't think of a better one. What about you?"

"Definitely," I replied. "There's no competition. Deciding to hike that trail was a great decision. I'd say it was easily the best summer of my life. And being able to hike it with you was special in a way I just can't put into words."

We finished the wine, watching darkness roll into the forest.

"I think life is going to be good here," Margo said.

"I think so too," I replied.

Many people told us that a long hike like this would change us, would have a lasting impact on the way we saw ourselves and our place in society. I discounted a lot of that talk. I had spent lots of time hiking and backpacking, and new the peaceful feeling that came from spending time in the wilderness. I thought when people talked about change that's the sort of feeling they were talking about. But spending so much time in the wilderness, with no other obligations and so much time for reflection, had a much more profound and lasting impact than I had anticipated. It had changed the way I viewed the wilderness, from a sort of gym where you went to prove your mettle to a place of peace and contentment. It had changed the way I viewed people and communities, as I realized that thru hikers and the community of trail angels and others that surrounds it are supportive and generous, with no ulterior motives. It changed my relationship with Margo. I knew she was strong and adventurous when I married her, but experiencing all of that, up close and first hand every day for 5 months, had really driven it home.

Hiking the PCT changed me in a lot of ways, all for the better. It was the best summer of my life.

Acknowledgements

There were an enormous number of people who helped to make my hike of the PCT possible. Without them, I wouldn't have been able to write this book. Thank you to Steve and Linda Tyler, my mom and dad, for help with logistics on the PCT as well as moral support. Countless trail angels helped us out along the way. Terrie and Joe Anderson, and Donna and Jeff Saufley are truly remarkable people who helped me and literally thousands of other PCT hikers through the years. Thank you to Papa Bear and Mountain Mama for opening up their home to us.

Thank you to Mihai Giurgiulescu and Laura and Gary Boggs for giving us a place to stay and some wonderful meals when we passed near your respective towns. Your friendship and support in the middle of our journey was priceless.

Thank you to the many trail angels whose names I either didn't get or don't remember for the rides, trail magic and general support. Just because I don't remember your names doesn't mean I don't remember everything you did for us on our hike.

Thank you to Dan Tyler and Linda Tyler for taking the time to read an earlier manuscript of this book and giving me insightful and helpful feedback.

Thank you to the Pacific Crest Trail Association for providing the infrastructure to make this hike possible, and for all the other wonderful things you do for the thru hiking community.

Finally, a very special thank you to Margo Contreras, who gave up everything to accompany me on this hike. Without your companionship the summer wouldn't have been nearly as fun, and without your encouragement this book would not have been written.

About the Author

Michael Tyler is a writer, adventurer and traveler. He received his Ph.D. from the University of Illinois in 1998. He has hiked, climbed peaks, and traveled around the world. Hiking the Pacific Crest Trail was his first long distance thru hike, and Walking Thru is his first full-length book. Michael currently lives with his wife, Margo, in northern California.

If you liked this book, consider taking the time to leave a review on Amazon. It helps others find this book, and I am interested to see people's thoughts on my work. You can also send me your thoughts at miketyler6@gmail.com. Thank you for reading!